The **Little Digital Video** Book

SECOND EDITION

A friendly introduction to home video

MICHAEL RUBIN

Peachpit Press · Berkeley, California

The Little Digital Video Book, Second Edition

Michael Rubin

Peachpit Press

1249 Eighth Street
Berkeley, CA 94710
510/524-2178
510/524-2221 (fax)

Find us on the Web at: www.peachpit.com
To report errors, please send a note to errata@Peachpit.com
Peachpit Press is a division of Pearson Education

Copyright © 2009 by Michael Rubin

Editors: Becky Morgan, Nancy Peterson
Acquisition Editor: Karyn Johnson
Production Editor: Tracey Croom
Copyeditors: Elissa Rabellino, Darren Meiss
Compositor: Kim Scott, Bumpy Design

Marketing Manager: Damon Hampson
Indexer: Karin Arrigoni
Cover design: Mimi Heft
Cover illustration: Mimi Heft; source images
from Photodisc, Shutterstock

Notice of Rights

All rights reserved. No part of this book may be reproduced or transmitted in any form by any means, electronic, mechanical, photocopying, recording, or otherwise, without the prior written permission of the publisher. For information on getting permission for reprints and excerpts, contact permissions@peachpit.com.

All videos used as the foundation of the included illustrations are © 2009 Michael Rubin, and are used with permission.

This book's content is based on an educational program developed by Michael Rubin, © 2000 and is also used with permission.

The video stills on page 105, and the author photo on the back cover, are by Lisa Strong-Aufhauser.

The mural "The Song of Santa Cruz" is © 2001 James Carl Aschbacher, and is reproduced with permission.

The photo on page 141 is © 2001 Studio 440 Architecture & Acoustics and is used with permission.

Notice of Liability

The information in this book is distributed on an "As Is" basis, without warranty. While every precaution has been taken in the preparation of the book, neither the author nor Peachpit Press, shall have any liability to any person or entity with respect to any loss or damage caused or alleged to be caused directly or indirectly by the instructions contained in this book or by the computer software and hardware products described in it.

Trademarks

Many of the designations used by manufacturers and sellers to distinguish their products are claimed as trademarks, Where those designations appear in this book, and Peachpit was aware of a trademark claim, the designations appear as requested by the owner of the trademark. All other product names and services identified throughout this book are used in editorial fashion only and for the benefit of such companies with no intention of infringement of the trademark. No such use, or the use of any trade name, is intended to convey endorsement or other affiliation with this book.

ISBN 13: 978-0-321-57262-2

ISBN 10: 0-321-57262-9

9 8 7 6 5 4 3 2 1

Printed and bound in the United States of America

For Jennifer, still my love.

Acknowledgments

There is no way for me to have a camera sucking up video from my immediate world without the trust and cooperation of my friends and family (many of whom grace these pages). Having me around often means being unwittingly dragged into my video obsessions. My deepest thanks to all my friends and neighbors who have supported this project, in particular: the Bryant clan, the Katz family, the Hastings-Quillans, the Blumbergs, Elmans, the Cree folk, Lisa 'n Kim, and all our friends who have tolerated my omnipresent camera, posed for photos (thank you Laura), and sat through hours of my video drafts with nary a gripe. You all rock.

A quick hug and kiss to the extended Rubin family who end up in my videos as in my life: Mel, Lorna, Gabrielle, Jacques, Joshua, Danny, Louise, Maida, Asa, Judie, Jeff, and all the cousins.

The book owes its roots to my *magnum opus, Nonlinear (1991)*, the first textbook bridging the gap between computers and film editing. Thank you to all my old nonlinear associates, particularly Ron Diamond, Ken Yas, Dean Godshall, and Gary Midgal. Special thanks to Adam Wilt—the consummate DV expert—for his advice and input.

I'd like to thank Nick DeMartino and my friends at the American Film Institute who encouraged me to develop this course, and have long supported my interest in education and my evangelical passion for this medium.

This book is also the product of my relationship with Peachpit Press. Thank you Lisa Brenneis, for my introduction there 8 years ago. I have terrifically enjoyed my work with all the editors (and my sometime coaches) over the years: Becky Morgan and Kate McKinley (for the original edition) and Nancy Peterson (for this latest effort). This book represents a positive synergy with Peachpit, and I value our collaborations. I'd also like to light a candle for Marjorie Baer, who worked with me to create this title and was always a visionary and supporter for great teaching in any form, and in particular, my somewhat unorthodox books. She will be missed.

Finally, there is the true source and inspiration for this book: my family—Jennifer, Jonah, and Alina, whose lives are so much a part of my own that any work of mine necessitates their profound tolerance and unwavering support.

This book was shot on location in Santa Cruz, Santa Fe, Beijing, Palm Springs, San Francisco, Gainesville, and St. Augustine. Any similarity to actual people and events is purely coincidental, except the parts about me, which are mostly true.

Table of Contents

CHAPTER 3   Shooting   **49**

CHAPTER 7   Finishing Up   205

Introduction

Results-Oriented Video

The goal of having a bunch of cool digital equipment is to use it. Shooting video all day with your camcorder is a waste of time if you never watch it—and if you don't edit it, you'll probably never watch it. You won't end up editing everything you shoot, but if you plan to watch it or show it to other people, editing will help significantly. Besides, editing videos is fun, if you set yourself up to succeed.

There are many ways to use a camera and editing software to make videos. Professional videographers—people who have the skills and equipment to make a living creating videos—pride themselves on owning tripods with fluid heads, some key lights and filters, maybe a few exceptionally high-quality high-definition cameras, and a lens set. They may also have a boom mic and perhaps even a digital-audio tape recorder they pipe through a small mixing console on the set. Videographers know about lighting and sound, and are very creative and careful at what they do.

But this isn't you.

You have a digital video camera and a personal computer. Today's camcorders are good enough to shoot videos for HBO, and your computer is more powerful than the one used by NASA to help put the first men on the moon. But making videos is not your profession. You do it when you have a little time on the weekends, and it probably doesn't get a lot of financial or scheduling allocation.

Our goals here—yours and mine—are as follows:

▶ To learn how to use your camera to get good video easily

▶ To shoot video that you can readily edit into projects

▶ To finish your projects

It is this last point to which I am most dedicated. Finishing your video is key. Your equipment can be so simple to use that you may try to do too much—shoot too much material or otherwise get overly ambitious—and you'll end up with a bunch of never-finished projects stacked up in your closet. That's no good.

Video Sketches

The process I use in this book is less about making "movies" than about creating what I call *video sketches*. Whereas a movie might be long, detailed, and highly crafted, a video sketch is more like a caricature—a gesture. A movie is often fictional; a sketch is deeply true. A movie is meant for a large audience; a sketch is just for you and your friends and family. But most of all, video sketches are easy, approachable, and quick. They may be a little messy around the edges, but I promise that you'll be able to do them on demand, and they will be full of personality and character.

To make a video sketch, I like to shoot unstaged moments—sometimes big, sometimes small, but all real-life snapshots from my immediate experience. Besides recording "events," an important part of making sketches is the capturing of tiny details and textures—the stuff that colors memory and adds a richness that is typically missing from home video.

I do no planning. There is no script, so I have no idea what is going to unfold. I don't even know if I will get enough good material to make a good video. I just shoot the best way I can. And then, like a kid after trick-or-treating on Halloween, I dump my bag of goodies on the table and see what I got.

Next, I take what I've shot—always less than 20 minutes' worth of material—and "pour" it into my computer (probably about 4 GB of material, so I've always got enough space on my hard disk). Then I edit it.

It's the editing that makes the video come to life. Unedited material, while it may be interesting only to me, is a world apart from an edited bit of video. Not editing is like enjoying the *ingredients* of a fine meal but never taking the time to prepare the dinner: It's sort of all there, but it's really not the same. A well-edited video is greater than the sum of its parts.

Within about an hour I have cut my 20 minutes of material down to 4, and it's pretty darn *OK*. If I have another hour, I tighten it up some more, smooth out the cuts, add music, and just generally refine it. I hold myself to a 2-hour limit for finishing the video, and just do the best I can in that time.

I use special effects very sparingly. For the most part, the only effects I use are fades and titles—maybe a couple of dissolves between shots—

but even these are minimal. I keep my titles simple and clear, and add them at the very end of the editing process.

In just a couple of hours, I have a great-looking 4-minute final video cut to a song with personal meaning. It's not perfect (we aren't going for perfect), but it's eminently watchable and enjoyable—even more so when the viewers are interested in the content.

Next I drag friends and family to my computer and show off the *finished* video. Each time I show it to others, I see things I'd like to fix. For this reason, I don't delete the video files from my computer right away—I don't post it on the Web yet, or burn a DVD; when I have a few minutes of spare time, I continue to tweak things now and then over the course of a few more days.

The moment I stop tweaking is the moment I begin to lose interest in the project. A few days go by; I've shown the video to several people and enjoyed watching them enjoy it; but soon other things in my life supersede this one in importance, and then I know that the time has come to end it. After all, I am not making a video for MTV or a Sundance Film Festival premiere.

At this point I generate a file of my video (relatively small, probably less than 100 MB) and upload a compressed version online to a Web site of my convenience. If I am particularly proud of my finished video, I also record the full-resolution "final" final cut to a *master* videotape and then delete the raw footage from my computer.

This is not the only way to shoot and edit videos, but I have found that it fits well into my busy life. And although I've worked on many kinds of professional projects, from TV commercials to theatrical feature films, I find this a good balance of effort and time for home-video hobbyists—it combines a little info from the professional-filmmaking world with a sincere understanding of the limitations that amateurs face. I believe that anyone can learn how to shoot, organize, and edit a video in about 4 hours. That's what this book is about.

Summary

Making home videos is a forgiving craft: You can be pretty bad at it, and they can still come out OK. With a camera set to automatic mode and some rudimentary knowledge of shooting and editing principles, you can make videos that are quite satisfying, maybe even professional-looking. And the more you choose to learn, the better your videos will be. As the solo videographer, you can expand your skills with the camera, with editing, with "storytelling" in general—your videos will just get better and better the more you do.

But for now, let's focus on starting out and work toward getting your first video finished.

You'll notice icons throughout this book. They are as follows:

NOTE: The Note icon accompanies text that is not essential but is still interesting or useful.

TIP: The Tip icon flags important tips or timesaving tricks that you would do well to learn.

VIDEO ONLINE: The Video Online icon indicates that the original video used in examples in the book can be found online at http://ldvb.blogspot.com.

WARNING: The Warning icon alerts you to something crucial.

The Basics

I hope you're reading this book before you've purchased a camcorder or editing system. Not that we can't work with whatever you already have, but I think it's important that we talk about a few fundamental concepts before you spend your money.

What's that, cowboy? Already got an expensive new digital camera? That's OK, keep reading.

Before you pull that bad boy out and start shooting everything you see, let's calm down, put the camera back in the box for a moment, and sit together to have a chat. Today's digital video cameras are so easy to use that you can do a great deal with little or no instruction. That said, you can also get yourself into a whole mess of trouble if you don't have a proper introduction to the subject. But don't fear: All it takes is a little discipline and a methodical approach to mastering this stuff. I don't have much discipline myself, and perhaps you don't, either—but you'll definitely need to get a few basics down before diving headlong into digital video. I promise to keep it brief, but I hope you'll at least read Chapter 1 before you flip ahead in this book. Deal?

Your Tools

NOTE: Years ago, I had a guitar teacher who played a fabulous Gibson guitar. His students all banged around on $25 garage-sale models, and we sounded like it. At the end of every class, he would borrow one of the cheap guitars from a student and just jam. I swear, he made our toy instruments sound unreal—a gentle reminder to us that spending two grand on a guitar was not as important as practice. (I still own my $25 guitar—and I still sound pretty marginal.)

It has been said that a great photographer can take great photographs with a marginal camera, but a marginal photographer cannot take great photographs, no matter how great the camera. Think about this.

To use this book, you'll need three main things: a digital camcorder, a computer capable of handling video, and software for editing digital video.

Your camcorder

For maximum power, ease of use, and flexibility, you'll need a camcorder that's digital, not analog (not that I think you'll even be able to find an analog camcorder anymore, but I just wanted to be absolutely clear).

Being digital today isn't enough. Compared with any time in the past decade, there is more to think about now when you go shopping.

This is a rough time to be buying a new camcorder—it is a period of flux in formats and storage media—and while computer technology always marches forward in a state of slow and steady improvement, camcorder technology is largely stable, with occasional tectonic shifts. VHS tapes were the principal consumer format available for more than two decades; then there was a shift around 1998 to MiniDV (tiny cassettes with near-broadcast-quality video). MiniDV continues to be dominant and important, but over the next few years tapeless high definition video (HiDef) will probably become the norm. It's available now, but as always, in periods of shift, there are lots of often-confusing and possibly expensive alternatives. Let's take a look at each of the options you'll need to consider when you're choosing a camcorder.

Standard definition versus high definition video: For personal videos, standard definition (*SD* or *regular*) video is pretty dern good. It was used by broadcasters and professionals for decades. Until recently, it set a high bar for quality. Technically, it is somewhat squarish in format (a ratio of 4:3, to be accurate) and has a resolution of 640 x 480 pixels in each frame. You can compress this video, but the more uncompressed it is, the better it looks. Simple, but now you need to consider a new option—high definition video (*HD* or *HiDef*). Broadcasters are moving everything to HD right now, at least in part, because any consumer can produce what used to be called "broadcast-quality" video. HD looks different from SD—there are around four times the number of pixels on the screen, and the screen's aspect ratio is about 16:9, far wider than standard video. More pixels makes it very large, consequently it must often be compressed, and there are many ways to compress it. Even professionals get confused. And while standard definition video is being phased out of the professional industry over the coming years, it's a heap of a lot better looking than the video you generally see on the Internet. That means if you're only ever going to post your videos to YouTube (for example), starting with SD video is probably more efficient than starting with HD video. Even though HD is very affordable today, it's still a premium product for a niche audience, and I think it's premature to jump into it on day one for your home projects.

It's always standard definition video (SD) unless it explicitly sports a high definition logo of some kind. The numbers that accompany this logo tend to describe the number of pixels in the image.

Recording media: Camcorders used to record on VHS cassettes. They were large and inefficient, and image quality was poor. Then came digital camcorders and the MiniDV tape format. And while there was some debate as to whether you'd shoot MiniDV or perhaps Digital8, it was all rather simple.

Now it is not. Not only do you have to decide if you want to shoot standard or HD video, but you also need to decide if you want to record on (a) a nonremovable hard disk inside the camcorder, (b) a special "mini" version of a DVD, (c) some kind of flash memory card (of which there are dozens of varieties), or (d) a digital tape, probably using a tape in the MiniDV format.

An unpleasant-but-typical array of recording-media options: some mini-DVDs, some MiniDV cassettes, some flash memory cards...

I checked with the professionals—people for whom money is really no object, but reliability and convenience are everything, and who tend to use a technology a few years before it's ready for consumers—and they are starting to move toward solid-state flash memory. I think this is a reasonable path. Tapeless work has many advantages (no timecode issue being a big one; no tape shuttling being another). But it still has drawbacks when it comes to organizing and saving material.

When you record on a cassette, you can always pull it out of the camcorder and drop it on a shelf. Later, you can quickly pop it in a player (or a camcorder) and watch it. It is inexpensively "archived" as soon as shooting is complete. Stick a label on it, log the contents in a notebook. All done.

With hard disk camcorders or flash memory, you can shoot a lot of material, but you have to clear off the memory before shooting more. This means copying the video from the camera (or memory stick) onto another device (a computer's hard disk, for instance) or going through an archiving process (by generating a video DVD), which takes longer than "real time." All of this makes shooting video less fun and more work, and I'm not all that happy about the technological "improvements" of the past few years. I am certain that problems will get solved, but today the excitement is left to those with lots of disposable income.

NOTE: I use the words camera and camcorder interchangeably throughout this book; and as the title indicates, everything we're doing is digital.

For these reasons, I'm steering you firmly toward the MiniDV tape format: DV (or HDV for high definition). They're excellent formats with a future of continued compatibility and are designed with consumers like you in mind. MiniDV achieves a remarkably good balance of cost, equipment size, image quality, and ease of use. If all you ever wanted to do was occasionally *shoot* video clips (but never organize or edit them into little movies), a good case might be made for choosing one of the other recording media. But we are members of the editing-savvy generation, and the small additional effort of using linear tapes is far overshadowed by MiniDV's natural capability to be automatically archived.

Look for a camcorder that explicitly sports a MiniDV logo, something like this:

Small icons that represent recording media options are on camcorders like STP stickers on race cars. The following are alternatives to the MiniDV tape:

Hard disk recording.

Memory stick recording.

MiniDVD recording.

Image Quality ("Chips"): Whether HiDef or standard, all camcorders come in two main varieties: *1-chip* and *3-chip*. The chips referred to—*charge-coupled devices* or *CCDs*—are video sensors that can "see" images and digitize them. They are the "film" in a digital camera. So what's the difference between having one or three CCDs? Image quality—or, more precisely, *color* quality. The 3-chip camcorders give an overall higher-quality video image but cost quite a bit more than 1-chip models—often three times more.

In my opinion, 1-chip SD cameras are plenty good enough for home video, and 1-chip HD cameras are impressive; 3-chip cameras are good enough for network television, and HD 3-chip cameras can output a feature film. Pretty much everything else about 1-chip and 3-chip cameras is the same.

Size: Make sure you choose a camera that is comfortable for your lifestyle, and small enough that you'll take it with you and use it. It should fit your hand, and you should know how to use its most basic functions. (At some point, though—and I'm loath to say this—you really might want to look at the user manual.) Chapters 2 and 3 lay down the ground rules for using your camera effectively.

Type of connection: How do you connect camcorder and computer? MiniDV camcorders generally come equipped with a special connector plug that uses a technology that is officially dubbed *IEEE 1394* but is popularly known as *FireWire* (Apple Computer's trademarked term) or *iLink* (Sony's). Whichever name it goes by, this technology does something nice: It allows a digital connection between your camera and your computer over which video can flow. You run a cable from camcorder to computer and then you can play the video on your camcorder and see it on your computer, and capture it there, if you want.

FireWire

NOTE: In addition to the *number* of chips, there's also the number of pixels on those chips. The larger the chips, the more pixels, and the sharper an image will be. For reference, 1/3 inch is a large CCD you might find in a pro-quality camcorder; 1/6 inch is typical for consumers. (If product specs don't mention CCD size or pixel density, it's probably small.) I won't offer an opinion about how many pixels you need for videotaping; all camcorders are pretty good. More pixels will generally cost you more money, though, and megapixels (a million pixels is a megapixel), are really only required for camcorders that double as digital still cameras, when you need to print images. Megapixels are important for print image quality, not for video.

As camcorders switch over to using tapeless media, fewer and fewer will use FireWire. While some have the USB-2 format for some uses, newer developments are separating the camcorder and the computer, and the only way to get video out of the camera is as *data*, not as *video*. The camera is recording not video, as you know it, but a set of large data files that can be viewed as video or manipulated as digital information. The costs of these tapeless media, and how you plan on the long-term storage of your video, must be considered when evaluating camera options.

Your computer

Both Macintosh and Windows-based computers can be configured to handle video. Macs especially are famous for their out-of-the-box "video readiness"; Windows PCs can do a fine job, too, although setting them up for video takes a little more dedication. Newer computers have enough processing power and hard disk space to run the necessary video-editing software.

An older computer may lack any number of features essential to viewing and producing video. Consequently, the cost of upgrading an older computer to handle video can often approach (or exceed) the price of a newer model that can deal with video right out of the box.

The speed of a computer's processor, or *CPU* (for *central processing unit*), is measured in *gigahertz* (*GHz*). The more hertz the CPU has, the better (and faster) the computer can handle special video effects and display images that have been processed in some way (*rendered* or *compressed*). Because we won't be delving into aspects of video that are heavy on image processing, however, you may not need as much CPU power for your videos as you might for, say, running games or computer graphics applications.

With this being said, more CPU power is really good for you if you plan to burn DVDs or work with HD. The MPEG compression method chews on lots of CPU power, and this is a core element of making DVDs or editing HD. But even if you shoot many videos, you're not spending *that* much time burning DVDs, and the small improvements in burn time you get with a high-end computer may or may not offset the higher cost of that hardware.

Computer manufacturers will always urge you to get as much CPU power as they offer—the truth is, you just don't need top-of-the-line horsepower for home video. Not anymore.

The storage capacity of a hard drive is measured in *gigabytes* (*GB*). All you need to know here is that the more bytes your hard drive has, the more video (and other data) it can store.

In terms of video data, there is a significant difference between SD and HD, and both can be compressed a little or a lot. Totally uncompressed, HD is about four times bigger than SD. But common HD compression actually makes for *smaller* data files than common SD compression. For instance, SD on a MiniDV tape doesn't compress your video very much, so it's only 4.5 minutes of video per 1 GB, and a 100 GB drive would hold less than 4 hours of SD. Compare that with a full-quality (consumer) HD video file; HD tends to run at 7.25 minutes of video for each 1 GB of hard disk (or flash memory) space. Thus, an 8 GB flash card would hold about an hour of HD video, or a 100 GB drive would hold 12 hours of HD. Strange, but true.

Look for specifications associated with your particular camcorder and format of video.

All you need to worry about is the minimum requirements for using your chosen editing software. New software applications and updates are released every day; always check first that your computer can run a program before you upgrade or rush out and buy something.

TIP: The only way to fit more data on a small storage device is to reduce the quality of your images, but I don't recommend it. You've spent a fair amount of money on equipment and, you're spending your valuable time making a video; don't get cheap and degrade the look of the video. When you embark on a shoot, strive to keep around 30 minutes to an hour of storage space available in your camera. In fact, having more space available is sometimes counterproductive, as you may shoot excessively, without discipline, and end up with lots of unedited (and unwatchable) video material.

Whether you're using a Macintosh or a Windows machine, your computer must have a *port* that accepts the camera's FireWire cable—otherwise you won't be able to hook them up to each other. Most computers come with built-in FireWire ports (they're often used for connecting to external hard disks), but look to make sure; in older models, you may need to install a separate hardware card to provide this connection.

Your software

For editing video on your computer, particularly when you're just starting out, go with a very basic software package. The technical term for what this software does is *nonlinear editing* (NLE). What it means, basically, is that the editing software is to video what a word processor is to text: It lets you easily cut and paste video sequences, adjust clips frame by frame, and control your camera's input and output.

But before you dig through all the product reviews in the latest video magazine, know this: Software choice is personal. Many brands of products do *about* the same thing in slightly different ways, and no one way is more "correct" than another. You just want to find an interface that you think is accessible and clear. You want to make sure that when your camera is connected to your computer, the software will control your camera.

Here's a good general guideline to follow when choosing your software: If it costs less than $200, it's more than appropriate for our purposes. *Simple* and *inexpensive* are the key words here—but again, be sure you get a feel for the software's interface and features, and go with a package that's right for *you*.

As of this writing, the best-known beginner software for video editing is Apple's iMovie, although new improvements to the software make it better for clip organizing and worse for basic editing. Not surprisingly, it runs only on Macintosh computers. If you're on a Mac, better perhaps is Apple's Final Cut Express—it can appear a little complicated at first glance, but for editing it's very nice. If you're on a PC, the software most comparable to Final Cut Express is Adobe's Premiere. I will say that Final Cut Express and Adobe Premiere are superb, but they're powerful and not all that intuitive; their features can be overwhelming and might keep you from jumping in right away. You only need to do the most basic editing. Of course, there are many fine (low-cost) consumer-oriented editing packages available for Windows, including AIST's MovieDVsuite, Ulead's VideoStudio, Roxio's MyDVD, and Avid/Pinnacle's Studio. Remember, this is an ever-changing field, and I expect that updates and new consumer products will continue to be released for many years.

(For more on editing and video software, check out Chapter 5, "Getting Ready to Edit.")

Other tools

You'll need to create a log book—typically just a spare binder—where you'll keep all the sheets telling you what's on each of your tapes. You may be tempted to maintain only an electronic log on your computer, but I think it's important to use a hard copy in a convenient notebook. I flip through mine all the time, and scribble notes here and there. I recommend keeping your log book near your

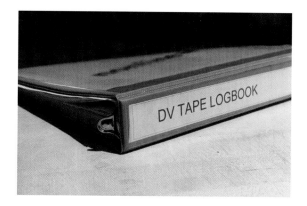

store of tapes. (For more on log books, including sample logs that you can use, see Chapter 4, "Organizing Your Video.)

If your videos will ultimately be shown on a television set, you may also want a *video* monitor—which is not the same thing as a computer monitor—nearby for full-screen viewing of your digital video. Sometimes I get so used to watching clips on my camera's tiny LCD screen that I forget how much better everything looks on a TV screen. A video monitor is not required, but it certainly makes for a better editing setup. If your life is devoid of standard analog video and you only watch on a giant LCD display, then you can probably get away with just watching on your computer. (For more on setting up your viewing and editing stations, see Chapters 4 and 5.)

And last but certainly not least, you'll need a starter set of videotapes. If you can get a brand that matches your camera, do it. Otherwise, simply choose a brand that's widely available, because (for technical reasons that aren't worth going into) you don't want to switch videotape brands if you can help it. I recommend buying a five-pack of 60-minute tapes. (For more details on these choices and further information about videotapes in general, see Chapter 2, "Your Camera.")

The bottom line

With as little as a $2,000 investment—for a computer, a camcorder, editing software, and of course this book—you can start producing your own videos. You can spend more for better tools, of course, but it won't change much else (remember my guitar teacher?).

If you invest in good equipment today, it should carry you through for many years. In time, of course, the digital video tools will change: Software will get revised, maybe becoming easier to use, having its bugs fixed, and becoming cheaper. Camcorders will offer more bells

Digital Videotape

Digital videotape. Why does this feel like an oxymoron? There is a very reasonable tendency to think of floppy disks, DVDs, memory sticks, and that sort of object as "digital," and think of a medium like tape as being analog. But this is wrong: It is possible for an old-fashioned medium like videotape to record and store digital data.

I think we tend to assume that linear media are slow and archaic, and therefore couldn't be digital. But the contents of a digital tape are still digital data. Both hard disks and videotape, in fact, use magnetic particles to store information. But the information on a tape, unlike on a nonlinear medium like a hard disk or DVD, must be accessed in a linear, orderly way. This is not unreasonable for a linear kind of data like recorded video, and it is economical for long-term storage of data. But once you get to editing, it is important to move the video data to a nonlinear digital medium like a hard disk, where you can instantly access frames that are separated by perhaps hours on a tape.

The key for a good consumer archive medium is that it (a) doesn't degrade or lose the data over time, (b) doesn't require too much special handling, and (c) is very inexpensive. And in spite of the importance of having video in a nonlinear format for editing and watching, linear formats will generally be far less expensive and more robust, thus tending to be better for saving in the long term.

and whistles in smaller and smaller packages. I also believe that the tape-based camera will eventually be replaced by some kind of *inexpensive nonlinear memory-based* alternatives, which will be great in terms of how you access and capture material with your editing system. But these won't be fleshed out for a number of years, and you'll miss a lot of life if you don't start recording before then.

Your Process

This book is divided into several sections—on your camera, shooting, organizing, and editing—in pretty much the order you'll need to know about them. But the truth is, *you can't shoot effectively unless you understand a little something about editing first.* I'll do my best to explain all this in an orderly way, but be aware that even though shooting and editing are distinct tasks, they're part of the same thing—*holistic video*—and what you learn about each part will absolutely affect every other part.

Preparation

In Hollywood, *preproduction* refers to everything that must be done before the shooting starts. This process, which can take months or even years to complete, includes writing a script, casting, getting finances together, planning out the shooting schedule, and so on.

For you, though, preproduction is a much simpler affair. All you'll need are your digital camcorder, a fully charged battery, and a blank videotape or two. You don't need to plan out the details, but you should be ready to think on your feet.

At home, I routinely keep a five-pack of blank tapes on hand. I keep my camera plugged into a battery charger almost all the time, and I bought the largest battery available—for about six hours' worth of power—even though it makes my camera heavier. By taking these simple steps, I rarely run out of either tape or power.

It's often said that luck is a combination of preparation and opportunity. So true. The key to great home video is always being ready to shoot. This way, when that "perfect" moment arrives without warning, you'll be on top of things.

Shooting

The word that professionals use to describe the actual shooting of the video is *production*. A major Hollywood movie can take months of continuous shooting to complete. Actors, locations, and equipment must be scheduled (back in preproduction), and the director typically leads a crew of dozens (or hundreds) to execute the filming.

Of course, your own production process will be on a much smaller scale. Your "actors" are friends and family, your video equipment fits right in your hands, and you try to shoot not a whole bunch more than you'll need to make your video. The key is to keep your production simple and realistic: Don't spend your time setting up tripods and lights, or even rehearsing shots, and make sure the shooting of each single "event" generates no more than 15 or 20 minutes of video. (For more on shooting, see Chapter 3, "Shooting.")

Editing

Although I refer to it as *editing*, this process is known in Hollywood as *post-production*. By definition, it encompasses everything that happens after the shoot, so it generally does mean editing. However, it also includes viewing and organizing what you've shot; creating log sheets for your tapes; handling any sound work required; adding any necessary special effects, titles, and music; and finally, preparing for distribution and release.

A home video usually requires only a few hours of this post-production work. First you put the video into your computer; then you edit and tweak it here and there, adding music, effects, and titles. Plan on a minimum of 1 hour and a maximum of 3 hours to handle all post-production tasks for your home video. (For further details about organizing, see Chapter 4; for more about editing, see Chapter 6.)

Finishing

The final step begins with distribution and release, which usually just means uploading the finished video online and posting (or emailing the link) for family and friends. If you're feeling like your video is extra-special, you can record your finished cut out of your computer and back into a *master* tape. Depending on your particular setup and needs, you may also want to record the video into other formats, such as on video DVDs. And when all this archiving is completed, it is the time to clean up your files—deleting old material from your hard disk, putting your source tapes into safe storage, and tidying up your workspace for the next production. (All of the finishing tasks will be covered in more detail in Chapter 7.)

Now that you understand the basic process and have learned a bit of the lingo, it's time to get friendly with your camcorder and start making your first video.

Your Camera

Ever notice how strangers can walk up to you on a busy street, even in another country, then hand you their camera and ask you to take their picture? It doesn't matter what language they speak, and it doesn't matter what brand or model of camera they have. You'll probably spend about 5 seconds figuring out how to use it; then you'll point it at them and push the button. Why can you do this? Because if you know the basics, you can take a picture with pretty much any camera. The buttons may be in different locations and you might have to ask a quick question or two, but no matter how fancy or plain it is, a still camera's basic functions are universal.

It's the same with video cameras. If you are familiar with the basics of video and understand how to make your own camcorder work, you can be reasonably comfortable using any other camcorder. This chapter, then, is devoted to getting you familiar with your digital camcorder. Not with all the fancy things it does, but with the absolute basics— what I like to call the "primitives."

Let's get primitive with your camera.

Fondle Your Camera

An important factor in making good videos is knowing how to shoot well, and the key to shooting well is knowing how your camera works. You don't need to know what all those little buttons do, and if you're like me it may be a while before you get around to opening the user manual. But you do need to recognize some major features and know the locations of just a few important controls (and be able to operate them while you are concentrating on other things).

Basic camera anatomy

Video cameras have many features in common. Here's a typical one:

Put your hand through the strap and hold your camcorder like you're going to shoot. Now locate the following items on your camera. (I'm sorry to say, you may have to consult the manual if you need help identifying any of them.)

Record button: *It's probably under your thumb, and it's probably red or sports a red dot.* The Record button is what you use to shoot. Press it to start recording, and press it again to stop.

On/Off/Recorder/Playback switch: *It's near or around the Record button, and you move it with your thumb.* Most camcorders have at least three *modes*: Recorder, Playback, and Off. Some units have additional modes, ranging from Standby to Memory to Photo. What I want you to focus on is switching between Recorder (that is, shooting) and Playback (watching) modes. This is an important thing to know, and although you will never really have to switch modes without looking, practice it without looking. (Smaller and cheaper camcorders can make this switching very challenging, so try it out when you're investigating camcorders.)

When the camcorder is set to Recorder mode, it is able to shoot video; on its LCD screen or viewfinder you will see an image that is coming "live" through the lens. Change the camera to Playback mode, and it is now able to play or move (*shuttle*) the tape inside. Notice that in Playback mode the *shuttle controls* (those familiar buttons for Stop, Fast Forward, Play, and so on) will be somewhere convenient. Find this spot. It may be on a panel along the top of the camera, or it may be part of a touchscreen control system on the LCD.

LCD screen: *It's folded down along the left side of most cameras (an unfortunate placement if you are left-handed).* The LCD screen is the one feature on camcorders that can most dramatically change the way you shoot video. Indoors—and pretty much anyplace where it is sufficiently dark—the LCD is ideal for seeing what you are shooting. Using the LCD allows you to move the camera away from your face, so that you can get more interesting angles (over your head, for instance, or at waist level). This is very important. Most LCD screens can

swivel around to be viewable from different angles—180 degrees with some cameras, so that you can view the scene from in front of the lens (see **Figure 2.1**). LCDs vary in size from about 2.5 to 3.5 inches diagonally; that may seem like a small range, but even a slightly larger screen can make a significant difference in viewing area, as you can see in **Figure 2.2**. The size of the LCD display is perhaps the greatest compromise you make when moving from a slightly larger camera to an otherwise cool pocket-size variety. Find the release latch and get a feel for flipping open the display and then snapping it closed.

FIGURE 2.1 Experiment with your LCD's range of motion. Don't force it, but apply gentle pressure until you feel it start to rotate. Most LCDs can turn all the way around so that you can see what is being shot from in front of the camera; this is called *mirror mode*. Shown is an LCD rotated to mirror mode—that's me taking a picture of the camcorder on the display.

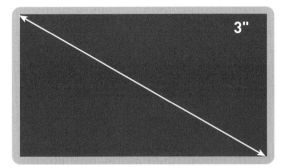

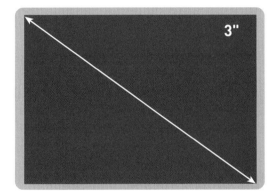

FIGURE 2.2 This is an illustration of LCDs at actual size. The first two LCDs are both 3.0-inch displays, the first wide-screen (16:9) and the second standard (4:3). The third LCD is also standard, but a different size. Notice the difference in screen area when you move from 3.0 inches to 2.5 inches. Unfortunately, larger LCDs tend to go with larger (and heavier) cameras. Wide-screen displays are measured the same way as 4:3 displays but are smaller in terms of area at the same diagonal size. They also have a perceptual decrease with the shorter height (you'd have to be farther from your subjects to see them standing, for instance). Viewing a 3.5-inch LCD is practically like watching a television; at 2.5 inches, it's just a big view-finder. Selecting the right LCD screen always involves delicately balancing your needs.

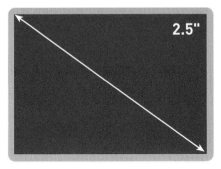

NOTE: OK, the LCD screen isn't all perfect and wonderful. Besides the screen's not being that useful in brightly lit areas (like outdoors), using it will burn through your precious batteries like crazy. Desire to use the LCD may just be the motivation you need to get a slightly larger battery for your camera.

Since 2008, more and more camcorders sport a 16:9 LCD screen. It's far more wide than tall. None of what you'll do here depends on which aspect ratio (*shape*) your camcorder utilizes.

Zoom: *This is either a rocker switch or a little slide bar. It will be located high on the camera and to the side; if you are holding the camera comfortably, it is likely under your index finger.* As cameras get smaller, manufacturers struggle to keep the controls accessible and simple to use. The zoom rockers on larger camcorders are the easiest to maneuver, but if you want a less bulky camera model, the zoom will be smaller and somewhat harder to control (see **Figure 2.3**). Practice zooming in and out; from not all the way out to not all the way in. Practice zooming slowly and smoothly. Practice jumping quickly from all the way out, to one or two places in the middle, to all the way in. Then see how slowly you can go from

FIGURE 2.3 The camera's zoom control should be its most convenient feature, ideally situated under your index finger as you hold the camera. On bigger models the zoom may be operated with two fingers and is oriented front to back. Controls that are oriented up and down are a little harder to use. Whichever way your zoom is set up, get good at manipulating it. This is the lifeblood of your creative shooting.

one extreme to the other. You will need to have firm control over your camcorder's zoom.

Tape carrier: *It's located on the side or maybe the bottom of your camera.* Every camcorder records on something, and you need to know what it is and how to manage it. If there is an internal hard disk (*HDD*), you can ignore this section completely; if it's a memory stick of some kind, it will have a slot you must know well; if it's a tape format, there will be a tape carrier.

You've got to be able to get tapes in and out easily and safely. With some cameras (smaller ones in particular), the tape carrier may be really well disguised. Find the Eject button, open up the tape carrier, and then look inside. Those little gears in there are fragile and precise, so never stick anything in but a tape, and always make sure the tape is oriented properly. Don't force it in if it doesn't want to go in neatly and smoothly. Also, of course, keep dust and dirt away from the camera's interior. I never even open a camera unless I'm in a relatively clean and wind-free environment. Pretend your camera is a living organism that must be opened up only in a sterile, hospital-like location. It may not always be practical, but it's a good way to think about it.

Closing the tape carrier is not always as simple as just pushing it closed. You will likely have to press on a small spot or an actual button to close *and lock* the carrier. If you push on the door itself, it may close a little but won't lock shut.

Finally, remember that one way manufacturers make these cameras increasingly inexpensive is by using more plastic and less metal in these small mechanisms, which makes them feel a bit cheap. If you chose to save money with a lower-end camcorder, you must be extra attentive to these fragile components.

TIP: Eventually you'll want to know how to set the controls to Manual. The two exposure controls to care about are Shutter Speed and Aperture (unfortunately called Exposure on most cameras). White Balance might be a third, but I would suggest always keeping this on Auto. Although entire chapters could be written about each of these controls alone, we won't cover them in this book. Instead, we'll focus on getting you through your first few successful video projects.

Exposure controls: *On high-end camcorders these are located pretty conveniently on the outside and maybe rear edge of the camera. On cheaper cameras, if they have these controls at all, they're going to be accessible from the LCD menu.* The exposure controls are the most complicated yet important features of a video camera. The camera probably comes with its exposure controls preset to Auto; keep them that way for now.

Viewfinder: *If it has one, it's located along the top and back.* The viewfinder is a little glass peephole with a small hood around it where you can put your eye and see your shot. With outdoor daylight photography, you may find that the scenes are too bright to view through the external LCD screen; in these situations, using the viewfinder is often the only way to see what's going into the camera. Most viewfinders are somewhat adjustable in position and angle, so experiment with yours to check its range of motion.

It used to be that all camcorders had a viewfinder; today only higher-end camcorders (or classics) have this feature. While they are occasionally important, manufacturers also know they are expensive to create—and by removing them, camcorders can be less expensive, lighter, and smaller.

The high definition camcorder (left) has a convenient viewfinder; the inexpensive standard definition camcorder (right) does not.

Display and Data Code buttons: *These may be located in the panel under the LCD (and are revealed when the screen is open) or housed somewhere obvious on the body of the camera.* On smaller cameras, to avoid taking up space on the body itself, these buttons may be accessible only from a touchscreen within the LCD. These "software-only" buttons appear only when you select the proper Function (FN) or Menu button to enable them.

As far as I'm concerned, one of the most critical settings at your control is for displaying code numbers over your video (see **Figure 2.4**). When made visible, the timecode number usually runs along the top right of the video display. Less important but somewhat related, the date/time features, when enabled, are typically found at the bottom left of the display. On my camera, the buttons that turn each of these on and off are labeled Display and Data Code, respectively. Data code, incidentally, can also be set to display the exposure settings for any piece of video recorded.

Data code   *Timecode*

FIGURE 2.4 Here's a typical playback on my LCD, with the Display numbers running along the top and the Data Code info on the bottom. Data code shows up only on the recorded video, not while you're shooting. Timecode, the number displayed on the top right, is important and can be seen while you're shooting or playing recorded video.

Lens Cap Wisdom

Detach the lens cap that comes with your camera and put it away. I don't endorse using the lens cap, for a handful of small reasons. First, you'll have to detach it whenever you go to shoot—only tiny lost moments, yes, but still a constant irritation. More important, I cannot tell you how often I have been shooting in a light breeze and the dangling lens cap either swings into view or bangs against me or the camera. Similarly, in my favorite "top down" shooting angle, the lens cap just hangs in front of the lens, requiring another hand to pull it out of the way. I say, *simplify*! Instead of messing with an opaque lens cap, I keep a clear UV filter over the lens. I almost never take it off. You can shoot through the filter, which arguably can enhance many kinds of shots while protecting the lens from fingerprints, dust, and other nasties.

The business end of the camera—take care of this region. Keep sticky fingers and sand away from it. Don't wipe it with your shirt. Use the proper materials whenever you clean it. I recommend using a clear, neutral UV filter as a sort of transparent lens cap.

Input/output plugs: *These are hidden behind a "secret" panel on the camera's side or bottom.* You will need these plugs—including FireWire (IEEE 1394 or iLink) or USB2, analog video in/out, and power—when you hook up your camera to other devices, such as for editing or watching your video on a TV screen. There may also be plugs for a headphone jack and possibly a microphone (mic). For now, take a look at them, just for fun.

Tape Playback controls: *You'll find them on the top of the camera body or on the LCD screen.* When you switch your camera to Playback mode, controls for Play, Rewind, Fast Forward, and other essential functions will inexplicably show up somewhere on the camera. As I mentioned before, all these buttons often won't fit on the bodies of smaller cameras, so they often use touchscreen technology to put "buttons" on the LCD screen instead.

Tape playback controls

All of those other little buttons and menus: *They're mostly buried in onscreen LCD menus, but occasionally they can be found on the top and sides of the camera body.* Don't worry about these functions right now. They do many interesting things, most of which we will ignore. For now, it is enough to know where they can be found.

Assignment 1: The Blindfold Test

Shooting video means operating your camera while looking through the viewfinder—or while looking at the scene. But you shouldn't be looking at the camera itself. At least not much. The more comfortable you get with handling your camera, and the more familiar you become with where all its important components are located, the better you will be at shooting video.

And so here we are: you, a camera, and a blindfold. (OK, unless you are a professional kidnapper, you may not have a blindfold handy. No prob; close your eyes instead. I trust you.)

Set your camera down in front of you. Make sure it contains no videotape. With your eyes closed, pick up the camera and get it on your hand, ready for shooting. Does it feel right and comfortable? Make sure your thumb can find the Record button and your index finger can reach the zoom.

Eyes still closed? No cheating. Now turn the camera on. You should be able to zoom slowly in and out, and move quickly between zoom levels, all with your eyes shut. With your other hand, flip open the LCD screen. Do this a few times, opening your eyes occasionally to see how you're doing.

Next, turn off the camera and then load a tape; then turn it back on again and shoot. Can you do it effortlessly?

Now, with eyes open, switch from Recorder mode to Playback mode; the control should be close to the thumb-activated Record button. Switching to Playback mode should be like tying your shoes—it should feel natural and instinctive. Make sure you note where the shuttle controls appear on the camera. Don't shuttle or press Play; just notice where these controls are, then switch back to Recorder mode.

Digital Zoom

Forget it. It's a trick, and probably a marketing ploy. Optical zoom is a true enlargement of an image using lenses and optics. With optical enlargement, an image has the same resolution regardless of how far or close you zoom in. With digital zoom, the camera simulates a resolution higher than mere lenses can provide by making the pixels larger. It is akin to saying that if you want a bigger image on your TV set, just sit closer. It's stupid, I've rarely seen it work the way you'd hope it would, and I've yet to meet a professional videographer of any stature who uses it. What you should care about is a camera's optical zoom magnification (usually between 8X and 40X), not the fancy digital variety.

Practice turning your camcorder on and off and getting smooth with the main functions—recording and zooming. This is the first step to shooting well.

Camera Care

Today's digital camcorders are pretty robust, and their prices continue to drop, but they are still relatively fragile and expensive household items. Even if you never drop the thing or bang it around, camera care goes beyond merely avoiding traumatic physical abuse. You will, of course, have to keep your camera clean and away from dirt and dust. But I don't want to state the obvious. I want to discuss some camera-care issues you've probably never considered.

Playing videotapes

The gears and motors that shuttle the tape are tiny and necessarily precise (see **Figure 2.5**). The act of shooting video is, in itself, not a particular strain on the little motors, but constantly fast-forwarding, stopping, or rewinding the tape can be.

FIGURE 2.5 A quick look at the stuff inside your camera—when the tape carrier is opened—reveals the record head (the angled cylinder in the middle) and lots of delicate tape-controlling mechanisms. Don't mess around in here.

There are two kinds of tape shuttling. One kind keeps the play heads pressed up against your tape, and the other retracts the tape away from the play heads before shuttling (see **Figure 2.6**).

FIGURE 2.6 Visualize this as you play back your video: The tape is all threaded against and through various doo-hickies and up against the play head. If you pull the mechanism away from the tape, the motor can move the tape much faster, and it has less contact with anything in the camera—it makes sense that this second method causes less wear on tape and camera.

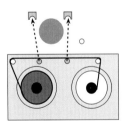

Cassette before loading.

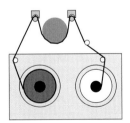

Cassette with tape threaded for play or record.

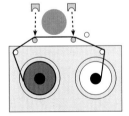

Cassette with tape partially unthreaded for fast shuttling.

When the camera's play heads are pressed against the tape, you can "watch" the video while it shuttles. This is both good and bad. On the good side, you can see where you are and know when you get to where you want to be. On the bad side, the tape will shuttle more slowly in either direction while the heads are in contact—thus, fast-forwarding is slowed from around 20X speed with no heads to about 10X with heads.

But what they don't tell you is that the longevity of a VCR (which is what your camera becomes when it plays a videotape) is measured in *head hours*—the number of hours the play heads rub against tape. The more you shuttle around with the heads on your tape, the less life your VCR will have. So, between overstraining those tiny, fragile motors and overtaxing the play heads, you should shuttle this way only when necessary.

Now don't get me wrong: Shuttling with the play heads on the tape is often necessary. As an amateur, you'll likely never hit a critical number of head hours. Nevertheless, heavy shuttling (with and without heads in contact with the tape) and constant direction changes will wear on the little motors and the delicate tape and can eventually demand attention. I like to think of all this like cholesterol: It's a basic part of your diet, and you'd never want to eliminate it totally, but too much of it probably isn't good for you. Moderation and mindfulness are about all you can hope for.

A long camera life

If you are worried about the lifespan of your camera and want to decrease the strain on its internal workings, here are a few guidelines:

First, get a high-quality camera. A good camcorder will probably last for many years and through all your shuttling around. By the time the heads wear out or the motor breaks, newer cameras will be on the market that are both less expensive and better than your old one. One possible reason for cheap cameras getting cheaper still may be that tiny compromises are made in the quality of their parts; thus they may wear out a little faster. (This is my hunch, and is also common industry wisdom.) A good-quality, name-brand camera will probably survive longer than a cheap, generic one.

Log your videotapes. If you keep a good log book or log sheet of your tapes, you won't need to shuttle all over looking for shots. A log can save you lots of time—and spare your camcorder hours of head time. We will discuss the whys and hows of keeping a log in Chapter 4; for now, understand that by logging your tapes you will also be taking care of your camera.

Headless shuttling. I like watching my video when I am shuttling the tape around. But to rewind a tape completely, or get to a specific location on the tape, it's better to press Stop (which pulls the heads away from the tape), and then press Fast Forward or Rewind (depending on which way you want to go). You won't be able to view the picture while the tape shuttles, but you can still see the timecode on the display, so you can use it to know when to stop. Shuttling the tape this way is also twice as fast, which is always a good thing.

Bulk capturing on the fly. I'll go into detail on this subject in Chapter 5. For now I will just say that this is my own method of getting video into the computer from tape: I simply grab all of my material in one or two big chunks. That way, I am not shuttling around, looking for little shots, asking the computer to rewind and cue up and roll to speed. Not every editing software package (or computer) can work with this approach, but it merits some consideration.

The Tapeless Life

For all the important reasons that I urge you to skip the tapeless camcorders, there absolutely are advantages, and one of them is that you'd be able to skip the previous few paragraphs as well as most of the rest of this chapter. You don't have to worry about tape quality and tape length; you can ignore most (but not all) issues of timecode and all issues of keeping timecode continuous. It's not that tapeless camcorders are bad—on the contrary—they just set you up for a life of video that doesn't include editing and archiving, which is what video enthusiasts may want to do. So for the serious home videographer, it's just too soon to endorse the tapeless life.

Videotape

One of the great advantages of smaller camcorders is the tiny size of the cassette tapes they use; six of them, roughly, fit into the same footprint as a single VHS tape. In coming years, standard *linear* videotapes may be successfully replaced by digital *nonlinear* media, which allows you to jump to any shot instantly. (While this changes the way you organize and store your videos, it has very little effect on your shooting or editing.) In the meantime, tape continues to be an *extremely* economical means of storing digital video, for amateurs as well as professionals.

I will briefly highlight two aspects of MiniDV tape here: tape length and tape quality.

Tape length

TIP: Rule of thumb: Buy 60-minute videotapes. (That means 60 minutes at SP, or standard-play, speed.) Never crank the camera up to LP (long-play) speed. The additional time you'll get isn't worth the reduction in video quality.

Considering the sophistication of this stuff, raw tape is actually pretty cheap. Manufacturers make videotape in lengths of 30, 60, and 83 minutes of recording time at SP or standard-play speed—which, I insist, is the only speed you should ever use. Since the cost is about the same for 30-minute and 83-minute tapes, sheer economics may pressure you to buy longer tapes and fill them to the brim. (If an apple costs $1 and a dozen apples costs $3, why not buy the dozen?) And many people do. But though they seem more economical, I think long tapes are more costly in the long run. Why? They waste time. Every time you shuttle a long-playing tape to find something—and you will shuttle your tapes often—the process takes just a little longer and makes the linear medium of tape that much more boring to use. Sixty minutes is the perfect length of time.

Tape quality

Cheap tapes or "high-quality" tapes—how to choose? The quality of a tape involves many factors: how strong the substrate tape material is, how fine the magnetic coating on the tape is, and even the process used for coating the substrate with magnetic oxides. All that said, don't sweat the tape quality for home video. Most tapes from respectable manufacturers (such as Sony and Fuji) will hold up fine for your uses and faithfully record the DV or HDV signal for years of happy video.

Using Your First Videotape

Get a tape that is 60 minutes long, and preferably the brand should be the same as your camera's. If that isn't possible, then at least be consistent and use the same brand all the time.

Before you pop a blank DV cassette into your camera, label it. Label it with an *S* followed by the date, written *YEAR.MONTH.DAY* (If you don't shoot very often, it could just be *YEAR.MONTH*). A tape started on Christmas Eve this year would therefore be labeled:

S 08.12.24

TIP: I try to use just the year and month, and avoid using the day as well, just for visual simplicity. But in cases where I need to use the day too, I will only add that to the top label, and leave the spine with the simple numbering.

The *S* stands for *source*, and it means that this is material you recorded yourself, raw and unedited. (I suppose it could also stand for *shooting*.) Every tape you own will have a simple label and a log sheet associated with it. You don't need to write notes on the tiny label that you stick to the cassette; instead, you can write notes on the big log sheet. For convenience in this book, let's call this first videotape your *S1* tape. For more on labeling, check out Chapter 4.

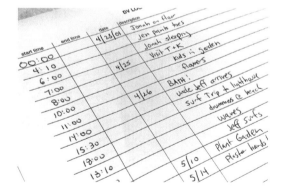

Labeling Wisdom

Over the eight years since I produced the first edition of this book, I learned that my original method of labeling (using an *S* followed by an incrementing number, like S1, S2, and S3, had certain drawbacks that didn't become evident to me until I had 200 or so videotapes. What began looking like the photo at left ended up looking like the photo on the right:

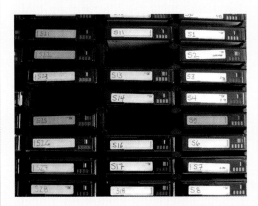 

The original method is ideal when you're very organized *and* you don't shoot very much. If you are missing a tape, it's obvious because there is a gap between tape S34 and S36. But if you ever lose track and stick a tape in the camcorder, and aren't sure what the last tape number was, you won't put a new number on, and this can spiral out of control until you have exactly what you don't want—lots of unlabeled tapes. This refined method makes it a little harder to find missing tapes but much easier to have every tape labeled, and also a bit easier to look for content even if your logbook isn't in front of you.

Load the tape into your camera. This may seem like the most obvious part of the process of learning to shoot, but I want to go over it at least once in a rather methodical way, looking closely at each step and the routines you may want to develop.

Whenever you put a fresh tape into your camera, always "bump" the Record button for a count of five. Record anything—your lens cap, your foot, a wall, the room you're in. It doesn't matter. You just want to get the tape rolling away from the beginning of the reel before you tape something that you might really want to save. The first few seconds of a videotape should be considered unusable, as they are hard to get into a computer.

Before you get all excited that you're actually starting to shoot, turn on one of the number displays on the camera if it is not already on. (If it *is* already on, turn it off and then back on again; it is important that you know where all the display controls are and what they show.) Onscreen displays may be distracting for beginners who are shooting, but they provide important information that we will discuss.

Data code, which we don't need right now, will generally show up in the lower left of the video display when the camera is in Playback mode (both in the viewfinder and on the LCD screen—and even on a TV set that might be previewing your video). Data code shows you the date and time that a bit of video was recorded. It knows this because the camera has a little clock inside; you'll need to set the clock if it's displaying the wrong time. Data code shows up only when you play back a tape, not while you record, so don't worry if you can't see it when you're shooting.

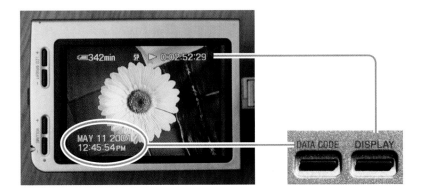

Display, on the other hand, is vitally important because it refers to a special number called timecode—data that is crucial to the future of your video experience, even if it's not obvious while you are shooting. Display often also shows you how much tape is left in the cassette and even how much battery power remains in your battery.

So turn on Display.

Assignment 2: Shooting Tape

Now let's make a recording. It may seem dull, but humor me and perform the following exercise as written.

1. Go to your bedside table. Things are sitting on it—a clock, some books, a photograph, perhaps a bottle of water. Now get into bed, act as if you are waking up in the morning, and shoot what you see on your bedside table. This is how I want you to shoot.

2. Without any big preparation, flip open your camera's LCD screen and press the Record button. While the camera is recording, notice the timecode count to :30 as you shoot the items you can see from your bed. *(Actually, it will count a little higher, since you bumped the*

tape for a few seconds before this.) Shoot close, zoom wide. And look around. But whatever you do, don't stop recording until you have counted 30 seconds.

3. Now do it again, only this time find each shot *without* pressing Record. Once that shot looks framed, press Record and don't move for 3 seconds. Then stop recording. Find the next shot and repeat the process. Feel free to move around between shots, but don't zoom or move—hold still until you press Stop. Shoot some close shots, then some wide shots. If you'd like, you can get out of bed now and shoot from different angles. Take about 15 different shots.

4. Practice shooting without looking at your hands or the camera. It's OK to look at the LCD screen, of course; just learn to work the buttons without staring at them.

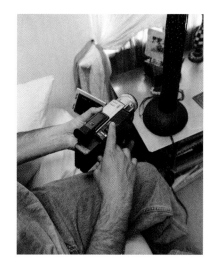

Now that you've recorded about a minute of video at the beginning of your S1 tape, let's talk about what you've done, and in particular about the timecode. We'll talk about the video itself a little later.

Your Friend, Timecode

Timecode is an exceptionally important and useful number. When a tape is recorded, a digital camera assigns a unique number to every frame of the tape and embeds this code number in that frame.

Good timecode makes a "where" on a length of tape. Without a steady code, you would be forced to shuttle around a tape scanning for the scene you're looking for. Timecode also allows computers to *understand* your tape.

TIP: If you've cheated and looked ahead, you may already know that many consumer editing packages don't care about timecode. Although this fact might make your life easier, it does not absolve you of your timecode responsibilities. Timecode is useful and good. It is critical for organizing and managing videotapes. Trust me here. Developing good timecode habits now will stand you in good stead should you move on to other (more advanced) video-editing programs in which timecode is a factor.

Timecode was invented so that people could easily find any frame on a long reel of videotape. It does two things: (1) It measures the duration that passes between two places on the tape, and (2) it gives every frame on the tape a unique permanent identification number. Timecode is the universal language of video, and it makes videotape editing possible. Most books, if they bother mentioning timecode at all, will not tell you about it until you are into the logging or editing process. But that is nuts. If you don't understand timecode while you are *shooting,* there is little that can save you when you get to editing—by then it's too late. So here at the dawn of your home-video career, we're going to talk about timecode.

Your camcorder generates something called *drop frame* timecode and puts it on the tape while the video is being recorded. You don't ask the camera to do this, and you can't control it. It just happens. The timecode always starts counting at 00:00:00:00 and goes as high as the tape length allows.

For timecode to be useful, and I mean *really* useful, it must be clean—unbroken and ascending. This means that no matter how you shot whatever you shot, the number must be counting upward without missing a beat (or rather, a digit). Having this type of code—and I will explain *how* this happens in a moment—gives you a certain set of powers and opportunities with regard to the tape you are recording. For instance:

▶ You can document what's on the tape, and where.

▶ The tape can easily be edited in any video-editing system, from the cheapest home PC to the most expensive professional setup.

Learning how to read timecode

Timecode is an eight-digit numerical sequence consisting of four two-digit numbers separated by colons, like this:

HOURS:MINUTES:SECONDS:FRAMES

00:00:00:00

Timecode the way professionals use it looks complicated because there are so many digits. Here's a real live timecode number:

01:02:36:18

This is read "1 hour, 2 minutes, 36 seconds, and 18 frames." Video always runs at 30 frames per second, so that "frames" part of the timecode number will start at :00 and count to :29, then roll over to :00 again. The rest is just like a clock.

There are a few reasons why you don't need to deal with all eight digits all the time. If you aren't working with long tapes, you might ignore the "hours" part. Many cameras also don't display leading zeros, so this further simplifies your timecode.

And when you're making notes to yourself about what is on a length of videotape (as mentioned previously, called *logging*), you need only write down *approximate* locations: **Minutes and seconds is plenty accurate**. You can make yourself crazy for no reason by trying to log your tapes to the frame! So even when I'm being *very* accurate, I log my videotapes like this:

5:10

That's 5 minutes and 10 seconds. If I'm off by a few seconds, I will still find the shot; and I really don't care about frames at this point.

NOTE: You might ask how I know this abbreviated timecode reference is "5 minutes and 10 seconds," and not "5 hours and 10 minutes," or even "5 minutes and 10 frames." The answer is only this: context. You will know.

Assignment 3:
Working with Your Timecode

Switch your camcorder from Recorder mode to Playback mode and find the Rewind control. Now rewind the tape you just shot (back in Assignment 2) and watch it. When you press Play, you will notice the timecode number at the top-right corner of the LCD screen. It starts at 00:00 and goes up. It was there when you were shooting, and it is still there, now permanently linked to the images on the tape. I want you to watch the material twice—once to just look at the video you shot. You'll be curious and it's fine to watch it. Now press Rewind and play your video again, only this time concentrate only on the timecode number at the top. Just watch it click away while you play the tape.

As you watch your video, you'll first see the bump you shot—a few seconds of pretty much nothing at the head of your tape. That's where the timecode starts.

Next comes the moment when you focused on the bedside table. Even though you stopped recording, moved, and started again, you will notice that the timecode keeps on clicking away without missing a beat. This is good.

Then, as the first shot ends and the next sequence comes up, where you were shooting the "still shots" and maybe starting and stopping a dozen times, notice that no matter how much you stopped and restarted recording, the timecode continues to count.

I also want you to notice that when you play past the end of the material you shot, the screen goes blue and the timecode disappears. It will look more or less like what's shown in **Figure 2.7**.

FIGURE 2.7 Compare the LCD screen when viewing *a recording of nothing* (black) with a region where *nothing has been recorded* (no timecode shows on the screen). Become very familiar with the differences here.

This should tip you off that the timecode is being added as you record video; it's not on the tape that you haven't shot.

Here is a graphical representation of the bits of video on your tape at this point:

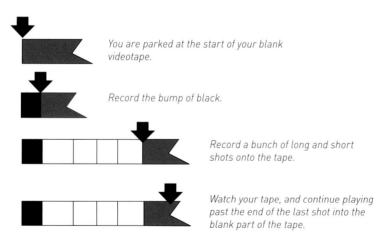

You are parked at the start of your blank videotape.

Record the bump of black.

Record a bunch of long and short shots onto the tape.

Watch your tape, and continue playing past the end of the last shot into the blank part of the tape.

Now that you are familiar with timecode, let's look at what happens when there is *no* timecode.

Assignment 4: Break the Timecode

Play your tape until you pass the end of your last shot and head into the blue. After a couple of seconds of this, press Stop. When your LCD screen goes blue, the timecode number disappears. Now switch back to Recorder mode and shoot some more. Walk into your living room, sit down, zoom the camera all the way out (as wide as it can go), and shoot anything you think is framed nicely. Don't move the camera; just hold still while you record. You are not only taping a scene from your house on this random day; you are also recording the ambient sounds in the house. While more or less ignoring the picture on the LCD, record the sound in your home right now, for about 10 seconds. Now stop recording.

Turn your camera back to Playback mode, flip the LCD screen open so that you can review what you've taped, and make sure the timecode shows in a corner of the frame.

Press Play.

You will likely see the last second of your recording, and then the screen will go blue. Without pressing Stop, press and hold the Rewind button. Watch the timecode numbers count backward as you rewind. You will see that the timecode for this new shot in the living room ended at 00:10. It started at exactly 00:00; as it continues to rewind, there is the little 2-second blue gap; then the end of the earlier stuff at the bedside table comes up, at a timecode of about 1:00.

Here is a graphical representation of what we just did:

You are parked in the blank part of the tape, after the last shot.

Record one more shot. It is "floating" in the barren wasteland of no timecode.

What you have just done is *broken* the timecode on the tape; the blue gap between these sections is blank—a barren wasteland with no video and no timecode. Avoid this situation at all costs. For the whole video thing to work easily, timecode must start from 00:00 at the beginning of your tape and continue unbroken, ascending, until the tape ends.

Why broken timecode is a problem

Let me give you a brief outline of the problem that broken timecode presents. Part of the way that computers "understand" a videotape is to know them by name (every tape has a *reel number* that identifies it), and every shot on a tape can be defined with a starting frame number (in timecode) and an ending frame number. The duration of a shot is determined simply by subtracting the timecode number of the first frame from the last. With broken timecode, one of the following situations could occur—any of which would confuse the heck out of a computer:

- A recording from tape begins at 05:00, lasts for 5 seconds, and ends at 01:00 (that is, the end number is "earlier" than the start number, yielding a *negative* duration).

- A recording from tape begins at 05:00, lasts for 5 seconds, and has *no* ending timecode number (you end in the blue; an impossible duration).

- Two different shots have the same reel number and the same starting timecode number.

On a tape with clean timecode, you could stop playback in the middle somewhere (say, at 20:15) and then ask the computer to find a shot that begins at 12:22. The computer would go find it simply by rewinding a bit. If the tape has timecode that starts and stops and starts again, there might be a shot with a timecode of 12:22 that starts *after* the shot at 20:15, and the computer would never be able to find it. Most of these problems arise when you are first moving your video from tape into the computer. Translating from one medium into another—even if they're both digital—is a vulnerable process.

Very basic video-editing software packages are sometimes designed to ignore timecode; consequently, any breaks in timecode won't interrupt an otherwise comfortable transition into editing. But professional editing programs will work only if the timecode is clean. You may be just starting out, but good timecode habits will pay off in spades should your interest in video grow and you want to graduate to bigger and better tools.

So one of the technical reasons to maintain clean timecode is simply to minimize potential computer glitches—and timecode problems can be a major source of glitches. But a more practical reason is that timecode simplifies many aspects of handling, searching through, and editing with videotape. If you ignore timecode for the short-term benefit of being more carefree with your shooting, your long-term success with video will be much less assured.

Assignment 5: Fix the Timecode

Let me be clear about this: You can't fix broken timecode. The only remedy you have is to reshoot the broken sequence over its current location on the tape. But what if you had shot an important, once-in-a-lifetime event? You'd have to choose between putting up with broken timecode and losing that crucial shot. Don't put yourself in this position. Just keep the timecode clean. Here's how to correct the broken timecode from the previous assignment.

1.   Make sure your camera is in Playback mode.

2.   Press Play.

3.   While you're watching the video you shot, press and hold the Rewind button until you get to the still shots you took by your bed.

4.   Let go of the Rewind button; the tape will resume playing. Watch the timecode numbers.

5.   Count aloud the timecode seconds as the tape plays. When it reaches the blue gap, the timecode will disappear. Remember the last number you saw.

6.   Rewind to get back to the recorded area. Then play it again, until the code gets to 2 seconds before the last number counted.

7.   Press Stop.

8.   Switch back into Recorder mode. The Playback controls disappear, and you will again see the live video coming through the lens. A timecode number is displayed on the LCD. *Now* you can record. Yes, you will be recording over the end of the last shot, but this is the only way to make the timecode continue from that spot.

9.   Shoot the living-room scene one more time. Hold still, frame your shot, press Record, and don't move for 15 seconds while you capture the scene. Note that this shot will be a little longer than the first time so that you don't leave any of the old shot "sticking out" under this new one.

TIP: Compare the two stopped frames in the LCD screens at right. No image appears in either one because the camera is fully stopped. But the stopped frame on the right has time-code, while the one on the left does not. Only shoot if the frame you're stopped on has timecode.

When you shoot, the only way to keep timecode continuous is to record over the end of the prior scene. If you are starting and stopping, turning off the camera, and then shooting some more, this overlapping will happen automatically: Camcorders are designed to back up a frame or two of the prior shot when they prepare to record. But if you go from Recorder mode to Playback mode to watch your shots, you must get back carefully to the end of your video before switching to Recorder mode again.

Summary

You are now ready to discover more about shooting video. Don't forget what you've learned about timecode—the subject will come up later. Also, make sure you keep the practice tape you are building. As we move on, you will use it again and refer to it periodically in our exercises.

Shooting

So now that you're familiar with the fundamental parts of your camera and what they do, let's see what you can do with them. This chapter goes over basic terms and concepts associated with shooting to edit. As you get more experience with editing, you'll be better able to shoot in a way that gives you the material you'll need. And of course, the more experience you have shooting, one would presume, the better quality of video you'll have.

The First Important Thing About Shooting

Shooting a video is not making a video.

Before the advent of digital video and easy-to-use software packages, editing was way too challenging for most folks. Consequently, the only way to get reasonable home video was to "edit in the camera." While this is an acceptable compromise in many situations, I think it's nearly impossible to get a satisfying video through in-camera editing: You would need remarkable self-control to shoot events in some sort of final order, and more important, you really don't know what's going to happen out there.

You shoot (and think) in a completely different way when you are editing in-camera, versus doing it with a real editing system. If you don't plan to edit, you will wander around shooting this and that—whatever

Not Everything Will Be Edited

To be completely realistic, accept the fact that much (if not most) of the stuff you shoot will never be edited. This isn't a bad thing. There are a number of reasons why you might not edit your video. Aside from your simply not having the time, it may be that the material you shot simply won't edit together very well. When you have a little more experience, you'll know almost as soon as you've shot something whether you missed too many key shots to make editing worthwhile. It's a fact of life. Still, watching the raw, unedited material is perfectly fun and viable. Just because you are shooting with editing in mind does not mean that you *must* watch only the edited video.

When you shoot to edit, even the raw footage you get will be more enjoyable to watch than whatever you might otherwise capture. In fact, you may choose to edit little videos, have fun presenting them, and *still* want to watch the raw footage at some point. Be comfortable with unedited video. There is nothing wrong with raw footage—and you *will* have a bunch of it.

you happen to see—and you will end up with lots and lots of boring video. When you shoot to edit, you need to keep in the back of your mind how you're going to get pieces of video that will look good when shuffled around and cut together.

Shooting to edit involves *nonlinear* thinking—that is, thinking "out of order." The last shot you make may turn out to be your opening shot when you put it all together. Movies and television shows are shot out of order, and for the most part, your videos will be, too.

Shooting to edit is like gathering bits and pieces of material you can use later. You are *collecting* video. You are *hunting* for video. Movies are made, not shot. And editing is how you make them.

When you take snapshots with your old still camera, they are just that—snaps. They are distinct and usually disconnected from one another. With video, your job is to take the DV equivalent of snapshots and assemble them into a little story (if you can): like a slide show, but with sound and motion.

Shooting to edit will be different from most of your previous video experiences, and it may be a little difficult to do at first. But once you start editing, you will get better and better at shooting material that is good to edit.

When I shoot, I am always quietly asking myself a series of questions:

▶ What's going on here?

▶ What in this scene interests me? What do I want to see more of?

▶ What little details would highlight this scene?

▶ What are my subjects experiencing? What do they see?

▶ What can I show of my subject that will remind me of my subject's personality?

▶ What would be another way to look at this scene? Can I get to that vantage point easily?

If I'm shooting a dimly lit scene, then my video will be dimly lit. I wouldn't want to turn on an extra light, for example, because that would change the scene—the moment—that I am trying to capture.

Editing creates emotion as much as video cameras capture it. The two work together, and you control both. If I am shooting a high-energy scene, like a sporting event or a party, I might want my video to reflect this energy. I might use many fast cuts, which means I'll need a lot of different shots. On the other hand, if I'm shooting a quiet, low-energy scene—bedtime in my home, for instance—I might choose long shots punctuated with close-ups to show the little movements that are missed in the wide view, and I would not use many cuts.

Rubin's Rules of Shooting

Let's start with some rules for making "video sketches." These rules are neither a political manifesto nor arbitrary. Rather, they are based on simple observations I have made that result in watchable and easy-to-make videos.

1. Shoot to edit.

   Shooting to edit means you are consciously collecting bits of video that you know will cut together nicely. You don't need any preparation for this (such as storyboards). But you must be dedicated to the notion that you are shooting with the intention of making a video out of the material you've shot. Keep it simple.

2. Ad-lib it.

   Create as you go. No script. No storyboards. No actors. No "loca-tion scouting." It's all improvisation. It's real life. Later, there will be time to shoot little plays you put together with your kids, or to produce fun little "shorts" or even a serious documentary on a subject that interests you. I do want to encourage your growth into these other kinds of projects, but they all take a degree of preparation and work that is fundamentally different from what you will be shooting here, making "sketches." For now, just look around and shoot your life. Go *au naturel*.

3. You're a one-person production team.

   Sketching a home video isn't a team sport. You must learn how to do it yourself. *You're* the one who is shooting, editing, and thinking on your feet. (Maybe your pals or family members can help you shoot once in a while, so that you can be in the video, too; but you must educate them as to what kind of shots to get.)

4. No equipment that you can't carry in your pockets.

   No tripods. No steadicams. Again, *keep it simple*. You *could* use additional lenses, adapters, or filters, but they aren't necessities either. You may be tempted by fun gadgets that make your camera big and heavy and sexy—but if they're difficult, uncomfortable, confusing, or time-consuming to use, don't let them get in your way. Shed the baggage. It's just you and your camera.

5. Use existing light only.

   Lighting is as much a part of a scene as the people and action in it. Adding light changes the mood from what is really going on (and it violates rule No. 4). Learn to appreciate the light that exists in the scene, and capture whatever you can just with your camera.

To follow this rule, however, you'll need to have good control of your camera (although automatic exposure settings make this awfully darn easy to manage). If the existing lighting isn't working for you, don't add light—learn more about your camera's manual exposure controls.

6. Concentrate on static shots.

By "static shots," I mean that the only thing moving is whatever you're shooting. Static shots are the building blocks of your video. Use moving shots minimally, if at all. In other words, stop moving around while you're shooting. This is probably the hardest rule to abide by. But you must trust me on this: *Stop moving.* Stop moving the camera, stop moving your body, and stop zooming in and out.

7. Shoot *real* moments, "small moments."

Take the camera out to shoot even if it's not a holiday or someone's birthday. Notice the way the light shines in your bedroom, or watch the shadows in your hallway after all the lights are out for the night. See the way a Popsicle drips down your kid's face as she slurps it up. Take a look at all the details you see so often that you hardly notice them anymore. Train yourself to really *see* these things—maybe to look at them in a different way. Now shoot them. In general, this means *candid photography.* These are what I call "small moments."

8. Don't let your subject talk directly to the camera.

Observe conversations, but don't participate. There are many ways to shoot and make fun videos, and interviewing people from behind the lens—having them talk to the camera—is one of them. But many of the rules of filmmaking, and in particular my rules for video sketches, don't work when people talk to the camera. It's simply hard to edit.

If you feel like interviewing someone, do it with the camera held to your side and away from your face (or set it down somewhere else), so that the subject is looking at you and not at the camera lens. But it's usually better simply to shoot people interacting with one another, not with you.

9. Impose limits on your project.

    This rule is critical. Shoot no more than 20 minutes of source video per project, and use this raw footage to create 1 to 5 minutes of "program." This way, you can finish a project in 1 to 3 hours of actual work, probably in one sitting. This is the nature of video: The more you shoot, the more difficult the project will become. If you keep your source material under 20 minutes, all the variables come together and result in exceptionally *finishable* projects.

10. Avoid in-camera effects.

    Ignore those little digital things the camera can do, like titles, special effects, and even digital zoom. Sure, they are fun to use—but *don't*. If you want effects, you can always add them later with the computer; if you use the camera for your effects, you can never remove them. So save the effects and titles for post-production.

How to Shoot

Shooting video is about learning to see differently and to think in a nonlinear way. Because digital camcorders are so light and small, and because the LCD lets you see what you are shooting even with the camera away from your face, you can take shots from a range of positions that would make a Hollywood camera operator envious.

Shooting, then, is partly about body positions and camera positions that are comfortable and stable. Periodically, you will discover the odd position that is neither comfortable nor stable. Trust your own limits and try not to hurt yourself getting "the shot."

Your body and your camera

In the old days of video (as it still is with photography), the camera was a mechanical extension of your eyes. It feels natural, therefore, to put a camera in front of your eye to take a picture. This way, unless you're squatting down or standing up on a chair, pretty much all your shots will be taken from about 5 feet off the ground, looking up or down from there.

Today it is much easier to hold the camera in any number of positions, from maybe 8 feet off the ground looking down, resting on the ground looking up (or 2 feet off the ground, looking straight ahead—nice for the vantage point of a two-year-old), or in front of you pointing straight down (for "aerial" photography).

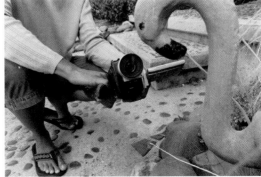

The closer you hold the camera to your body, the more supported it is and the more stable the images will be. If you can grip the camera solidly in your right hand—unfortunately, these things are not well designed for lefties—you can have a good range of motion and use your left hand only to adjust the LCD's angle and to stabilize the camera.

Once you've got it held securely in your right hand, you really need only your thumb and a finger to operate the camera, regardless of its size: your thumb on the Record button and your index finger on the zoom control.

But to get shots with the camera in a different position relative to your body, you can also hold the camera securely in your *left* hand, and use your *right* hand alone to press the Record button and to zoom. This allows for a different range of positions, from shooting back toward yourself (if you want to be in a shot) to very low in front of you. Experiment with all the positions of your camera and its LCD, and experience how this flexibility allows you to move the camera around.

Think like a wildlife documentarian

Ever wondered how those documentary photographers get that incredible footage of a certain animal walking right up to the camera, eating a particular bug right in focus, and then scampering away?

I once asked a famous wildlife documentary producer what the trick was.

"Patience," he said. He explained that you have to know where to set up, and be familiar with your subject matter. "Set up, let the animals get used to you—your smell, the camera—until they don't care and get on with their business." And ultimately, this kind of filmmaking uses up lots of footage; you can't wait until something happens to turn on the camera. You have to be shooting *before* something happens so that when it happens, you've got it. Get it?

Because you plan to edit your footage, and DV tape is relatively inexpensive, you can get great shots simply by getting in the right spot, turning on the camera, holding still, and waiting. Be patient. Let the camera roll. Sometimes this is the best way to let something unfold on camera. For you, being patient doesn't mean hours, but it sometimes might mean minutes (it sounds short, but it is difficult holding still for even a minute or two without getting a little antsy).

Keep in mind that it takes about 7 seconds to start shooting video from a camera that is turned off. You can miss a lot of activity in 7 seconds. It even takes about 2 seconds to start recording video from a camera that is turned on but not currently recording. (Admittedly, tapeless alternatives like HDD and memory Sticks start recording a little faster.) Consequently, it can be cheaper and more efficient to keep shooting while *anticipating* that something cool will happen. But be aware: This means that you're looking through the lens to see things, which often leads to recording a lot of bad material.

Zooming and scanning around are ways to move the camera from one "shot" to another, but the material recorded during these moves and zooms should be considered no good—just garbage recorded as you move from shot to shot.

Before we delve into the kinds of things you'll be shooting (and what you will see through the lens), I want to talk a little about storytelling.

Structure

Editing is about creating a structure from a bunch of images. But the images aren't random; they are chosen by you. While you can make a decent video with very little structure in the shots you record, having a little structure during your shoot goes a long way.

The fundamental elements of structure—of storytelling—will likely be familiar to you. When shooting video you will need the following:

▶ Beginning material

▶ Main action or event material

▶ Ending (closure) material

Realize that these aren't the only ways to look at the elements of a video. The structure could be like a joke (setup and punch line), or it could be like a movie (introduction, conflict, climax, resolution). But I think it's simplest to think of it in terms of a beginning, middle, and end.

When you shoot a video, there are any number of ways you might approach it. If you are thinking ahead, you might shoot the beginning material first. Let's say you're going on a road trip. As you get your camera out, you think: "I've got only one chance to shoot everyone preparing for this trip, so I'd better get it now." That's an introductory moment. But other times something will just happen, and you'll pull

NOTE: Standby mode: To conserve precious battery juice, cameras usually turn themselves off if you don't use them for a few minutes. Standby mode is a great feature for the most part, but it can be a little confusing at first—and downright irritating later on. There you are, looking at the world through the viewfinder, waiting for just the right shot, and then—blam—the camera shuts itself off. The only way to get it turned back on is actually to switch it off and then on again.

VIDEO ONLINE: Watch an example of a highly structured video online: http://ldvb.blogspot.com—look for Sketch A.

the camera out and start shooting. You may not have a chance to think about what "introduces" this event until after the moment is past. But that's OK. Editing allows you to shoot out of order.

Let's look at the structural (storytelling) elements of a video, in the order they usually occur for your shoot.

Middle shots: The action or event

Usually, something is going on that makes a bell go off in your head: "Go get the camera!" You are responding to a special action or event, and you (understandably) want to capture it on tape—for instance:

- ▶ Your kid is doing something cute.
- ▶ Friends from out of town show up.
- ▶ Some unusual or newsworthy moment unfolds before you.
- ▶ There's a birthday party.
- ▶ Your dog inexplicably whistles "The Battle Hymn of the Republic."

You see something happening, you grab your camera, and you shoot. The middle action scenes are the most obvious ones to shoot. They are probably why you are shooting in the first place, so I don't need to remind you to do so. You will want to "cover" the scene with wide shots, close shots, and medium shots (more about the different camera shots later).

Beginning shots

You need to find a beginning to your video. It may be one shot long or a short sequence of shots. You never know what will make a good beginning, but if you think about it while you are shooting, you may find many elements that gently lead viewers into the little story you are about to tell them.

If you just can't find a beginning moment, there are ways to work around it while editing. But having a beginning will always make the completed project look more professional and more accessible to the people watching it.

A beginning shot might be a clock changing time and an alarm going off; it might be a lone car driving up to a house on a quiet morning; it can be a sunrise. It can be any little thing that foreshadows the events that will happen next.

Ending (closure) shots

At the same time that you are thinking about beginnings, it's a good idea to look for endings, too. Closure shots keep videos from just stopping in a manner that is often referred to as "cold." I enjoy hunting for endings more than beginnings. Remember that the closure material will be the last thing your viewers see, so it should have

lasting-impression value. A cool ending can make the video. It's like the punch line for a joke.

Of course, there are the classic but rather clichéd ending shots—turning out a light, closing a door, waving good-bye, or walking into the sunset—and I have used all of them. (They may be clichés, but good endings are really all in the execution anyway, so if you're going to use a cliché, try to do it in a personal way!) Many images scream out "ending." Any time people are walking away from the camera, you have a nice closing shot. It can be as simple as the look on someone's face after he blows out his birthday candles or completes the jump or tucks the kids in for the night. Each of these events might be closed out with a single, close-up shot of that satisfied face.

One particularly nice result of keeping the camera still is that people will be entering and leaving the frame. Someone exiting the frame—and the resulting still-life shot that remains—is a fine and classic way to close out a video.

Now that you are thinking a bit about structure, let me define the basic ways a camera frames the world. These are the raw ingredients of a video.

Camera Shots

In Hollywood, camera shots are generally described in terms of how large or small the subject is in the frame. When the subject fills the screen, it's a close-up. When the subject is far away, it's a wide shot. There are no hard rules about when a close-up gets far enough away to become a medium shot, and when a medium shot becomes a wide shot. It doesn't really matter what a shot is called—these terms are just a convenient way to describe the framing of images.

With professional (that is, really expensive) cameras, the way you change a shot is often by changing the lens. To get up close, you put on a lens with a higher magnification. To make everything seem farther away (and to see more stuff in the frame), you change to a wide-angle lens.

Consumer camcorders generally do not have changeable lenses. Instead, they provide a very powerful zoom lens that gives you remarkable ability to change the magnification level quickly, without actually changing the lens itself. Think of your zoom lens as a *bag of lenses*, any of which you can pop on your camera any time.

Let's discuss your camera shots and how you might use them.

Fundamental Shot Vocabulary

CU   Close-up

MS   Medium shot

WS   Wide shot

These are the three basic shots, but there are lots of variations. For instance, *MCU* means "medium close-up," and *ECU* means "extreme close-up."

The close-up (CU)

The close-up shot can be described in one word: *powerful*. Filling the screen with your subject is raw, intense, in your face. It's like spicy food—you don't want too much of it, just enough for some flavor, to satisfy. Use close-ups carefully (movies use them relatively infrequently, and TV uses them only a little more often), but don't forget to use them, either.

The good news about close-ups is that they are full of detail and can be really lovely. Also, they almost always appear out of context—disembodied, disjointed, and sometimes surreal. A video of nothing but close-ups would be extremely hard to watch; the viewer would need to step back to see what we are looking at so closely. Close-up shots are perfect *inserts* (more about these and other special shots later). They have many uses throughout the making of the video, but they are essential when you need something to let you cut away from one shot before going on to the next.

The bad news about close-ups is that because your camera's viewfinder and LCD are so small, there is a real tendency to shoot *everything* too close. Remember that your video is supposed to be viewed on a TV set, so you must shoot with that in mind.

TIP: When you're shooting someone's face, don't be afraid of cutting off the top of her head. It's the eyes, not the head, that make for a powerful close-up of a person.

The medium shot (MS)

Getting good medium shots can be difficult with the camcorder's zoom controls. You end up either zooming in all the way (for a close-up) or zooming out all the way (for a wide shot). But don't forget the medium shot. It should be your bread and butter. A medium shot of a person will frame the entire head, as well as a good part of the shoulders and maybe some of the torso. Once you can see the subject's feet, of course, you've strayed from "medium" and gone into wide-shot territory. Because a video frame is always horizontally oriented, and because people are generally vertical—that is, not lying down—when you're shooting them, there will be a fair amount of space around a person framed in a medium shot. These are good situations for applying the *rule of thirds* (discussed in "Framing and Design," coming up). On the other hand, a medium shot will nicely fit two people side by side; this type of medium shot is also called a *two-shot*.

NOTE: Medium shots are perhaps the most negatively impacted by the use of wide-screen (16:9) displays, as the vertical height of the frame is shortened, and you'd need to be slightly farther away from your subjects to fit them in the frame. Because medium shots are a little harder to create in wide screen, you must be that much more familiar with seeing and shooting them.

A medium shot lets viewers feel as if they're seeing your subject up close, but it is not as intimate (or as invasive) as a real close-up shot. Most shots in movies and TV are medium.

Practice getting your camera into the medium-shot range. Once you are comfortable with it, the MS is extraordinarily handy: You don't feel pressure to move the camera because the people you're shooting have room to move around in the frame and not exit. You'll be surprised at how much expression and detail you can capture in a medium shot.

It's worth noting that you might have medium shots that aren't of people. This medium shot is a simple cutaway; however, you can imagine that you could catch this same subject matter from the same camera position, but in a close-up (just the flower petals) or wide shot (the entire room).

The wide shot (WS)

A wide shot contains a lot of information. Even objects that are moving appear to move more slowly when they are far away from you. Therefore, it is important that you hold very still and let wide shots just sit there a little longer than you might for a closer shot. Because subjects tend to be smaller in the wide shot, and because there are more little things here and there, viewers will need a little time to figure out what they are looking at and to scan the scene. A close-up can be "read" in a fraction of a second, but a wide shot that lasts only a second is useless.

Wide shots are exceptionally important, not only to balance out the close-ups but also to let the audience understand where the scene is taking place—the context of your shoot. And when you get to editing, the wide shots give you material for pacing; they allow the viewer to relax for a moment and take a breath. Although they are critical throughout the shoot, wide shots (in the form of the *establishing shot*, discussed later) are essential elements to both beginnings and endings.

Wide shots are also the easiest ones to forget, because they look boring on an LCD. But they are much nicer on a TV screen, so don't forget to shoot them. Just be patient—and hold still.

These are actually more than wide shots; they are *extreme wide shots* (EWS), where the subject is particularly small in the frame.

Depth of Field

Depth of field relates to how much of an image is in focus in your frame, and is related to how close or far you are from a subject, as well as the lens's focal length (wide angle versus telephoto). Thus, your subject could be the same size in two different frames, but the background would be in focus in one and blurry in the other (see **Figure 3.1**). When you're getting started, don't worry about controlling depth of field: it can be a little complex and there will be ample time later to explore it.

FIGURE 3.1 On the left are flowers shot from a distance, using telephoto. Notice that they are about the same size in the frame as the flowers on the right, which I shot while sitting right next to them, using wide angle. Both shots are close-ups; the one on the left has a very short depth of field (the background is blurry) compared with the one on the right (where even the far background remains in focus). Short depth of field tends to give video a more filmlike look, which often is appealing.

NOTE: *Close-up* and *wide shot* do not directly correlate with high magnification and low magnification (often labeled on cameras as T for "telephoto" and W for "wide angle," respectively). You can have a wide shot—say, a mountain range in the distance, with tiny-looking cars traveling up a deserted highway—using the camera at its maximum magnification. Similarly, some of my favorite close-ups are not zoomed in tight; rather, I just sit really close to the subject I am shooting. The difference between these situations may not be obvious, but it involves an optical property called *depth of field*.

Coverage

Coverage is a term from Hollywood that refers to making sure you record enough material—and the right kind of material—that you can edit something out of it.

Coverage is often described in terms of the camera shot used (like wide or close), as well as the structure (like beginning shots). But coverage means more than that. When you shoot something, you should have a sort of casual checklist in your head. This is what it would say:

- ▶ Establishing shots
- ▶ Cutaways
- ▶ Shot/reverse shots
- ▶ Over-the-shoulder (OS) shots
- ▶ Point-of-view (POV) shots
- ▶ Top-down shots

You'll likely need some of each of these shots in your video. The fewer shots you have in a particular category, the harder it might be to edit your footage into something cohesive.

Let's examine each of these coverage types and how you can wrestle them from defiant opportunity. Finding each of these pieces in the natural flow of life that unfolds before your lens will take practice, but it will get easier in time.

The establishing shot

Establishing shots are usually, but not always, associated with the beginning of a video.

Every video must begin somewhere. Every TV show starts out with opening credits, which often establish where we are and what kind of mood we're supposed to be in. They often include a cityscape or the exterior of a building or the house where the main characters live—some kind of local (outdoor) shots to balance the entire program shot on a set indoors. The establishing shots need not be big panoramas or even superwide shots; they just need to be wide enough to establish where the action is taking place.

Establishing shots answer the pressing question, *Where the heck are we?* You probably started shooting on the main action and maybe aren't even sure how you got here, but don't forget to get some shots establishing a place in space and time.

Here are some establishing-shot tips:

▸ If you're shooting an event, think about how you got there. (Did you wake up early? Pack up? Drive?)

▸ I like to shoot clocks to establish a time, and sometimes I use snippets of CNN or a national newscast—I just record the TV screen for a moment—that might place us in a unique timeframe.

▸ If you are shooting inside a house or other building, can you also capture any action from the outside? Sometimes, during an indoor party I will quietly go outside my house, stand in the street or driveway, and shoot a little "voyeur" footage through a window. Thus, I start with a wide shot of the house; then move in closer and shoot through the window, where I can see something going on; and finally go back inside, and it's a natural to shoot more of the party itself. (I can always decide on the order of these scenes during the editing, since it could work in any number of ways.)

Using Signage

One trick in establishing time and place is to incorporate the signs, logos, and other graphics that are "indigenous" to the scene. So, rather than beginning a video with the title "Our Day at the Zoo," it can be much cooler to include a shot of the zoo's entrance sign. Indigenous signage is useful for establishing your settings, and it adds some local color besides.

▶ If you're shooting a child doing something, see if you can find a vantage point where you can hear the action before you see it—say, starting in another room and sensing that something is happening nearby. This technique serves a dual purpose: It establishes where we are, and it makes the viewer curious as to what is about to happen.

The shot/reverse shot

The shot/reverse-shot concept is critical to producing editable footage. It is not one shot but two shots that have a special relationship to each other—a natural pair that often are the central elements of an edited sequence. It means, simply, that if I shoot something from here, I need to remember to walk over there and shoot it from the other side. In technical terms, you'll need to draw an imaginary line with your eye between you and whatever you are shooting. I stand and shoot from a particular spot until I'm satisfied that I have a few minutes' worth of my subject. Now comes the important moment: I turn off the camera, walk to the other side of the subject (keeping slightly on this side of 180 degrees if I can), and then shoot facing back toward where I was standing before. If I'm shooting two people talking or interacting, the imaginary line is between them, and I need to shoot from one side and then the other (see **Figure 3.2**).

Not every shot demands a reverse. If I can see everything I want to see from the first vantage point, then moving to the other side is pointless. Very often I'm satisfied with the content of a shot from the particular place I'm standing, even if I'm aware a reverse would give me an additional viewpoint. Getting a reverse on something intensifies the importance of that moment. When you give the audience such a complete (magically omnipresent) viewpoint, a small moment can be exaggerated into an "event."

Let's say that two people are talking face-to-face. I could stand at their side, seeing two profiles, and shoot them as they talk, in which case I don't really need the reverse. Now, let's say I choose instead to shoot from behind one of the people, so that I can see one person's back and

FIGURE 3.2 This funky top-down view illustrates the basic positioning required to get a shot and then the reverse. To make an aesthetically pleasing reverse shot, the idea is that you shouldn't cross "the line"—meaning the imaginary line between the two people talking. When you shoot them, you're just to the side of that line, and when you go to get the reverse, you're still a little bit on the same side of the line. By not crossing the line, notice that the subjects remain in the same relative position in the frame (the baby is on the left and the guy is on the right in this example), which makes the edits back and forth flow nicely. It's a distracting concept for some people, and if you ignore it until you're more comfortable with shooting, that's OK.

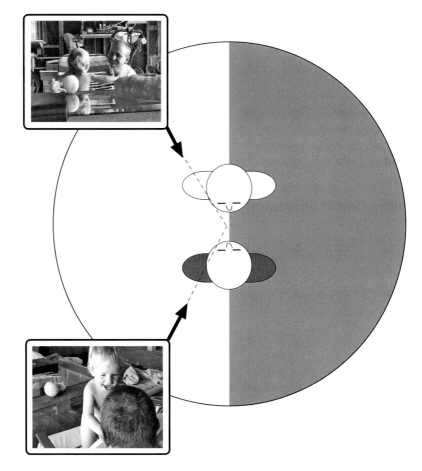

the other's face. For this shot, I will want to get the reverse, so that we get a look at both their faces. Once edited, this kind of shot coverage can give a very sophisticated look to your videos.

For example, the day my son first crawled, I sat on the floor with him and shot quite a bit of video. A reverse of this shot would be difficult. Not only is my son against a wall, but there really isn't anything to "reverse to" (see **Figure 3.3**).

FIGURE 3.3 I recorded one long (5-minute) shot of my son as he crawled. I set him on the floor, put the camera down there with him, and let it roll. Here are a few moments from the shot.

Then again, this isn't totally true: He's not alone in the room. Although I am only there to shoot him, the special moment I'm capturing is partially about me watching it unfold—and thus I came up with the idea to cheat a reverse (see **Figure 3.4**).

FIGURE 3.4 With my son out of the room (off with his mom down the hall, I think), I have set the camera on the floor where he was crawling and am shooting back toward myself, posing and "faking" watching him. I'm trying to do pretty much whatever I did when he was here, except now I'm not holding the camera.

NOTE: Sometimes the reverse shot of someone doing something is of *you*. You have two choices in this situation: the "real" reverse, which would show you with a camera but is impossible to do with just one camera; or a "cheated" reverse, where you put the camera where the subject was, go back to where you were watching from, and have the camera shoot back toward you— but not with a camera. (It's called a *cheated reverse* because, of course, it didn't really happen this way. If the ethical implications of this cheating cause you concern, just don't do it.)

VIDEO ONLINE: Take a look at Sketch B on the Little Digital Video Book blog: http://ldvb. blogspot.com.

The over-the-shoulder (OS) shot

If I shoot your head in a medium shot, there is a big difference between a *single* (just you) and an OS (which includes the edge of the person you are interacting with). Notice:

NOTE: When you describe a shot as OS in any written notes, make sure you note whom the shot is of. For example, "OS Mike" means you're looking over someone's shoulder toward Mike.

When the foreground contains a shoulder (or a bit of the back of a head), we can feel the relationship between the people in the video. When it isn't there, it's as if the person you're shooting is talking alone, which isn't really the case. Close-up shots can look too crowded with something in the foreground, but medium shots are very nice with the subject framed by a (sometimes unlit, out-of-focus) shoulder of another person.

OS shots are excellent for use in conjunction with the classic shot/reverse-shot method, which means that if you shoot OS, the reverse shot is also ideally another OS. But even if you don't intend to get the reverse, the OS is a cool element to incorporate in your videos.

OS shots are quite common in movies and television shows—so common, in fact, that I'm surprised I had never really noticed them before someone pointed them out to me. Now I see them everywhere.

This is another sort of OS shot (at left), but it isn't of two people and couldn't have a reverse; whereas you might shoot close (of just the hand painting), the OS version also helps establish the relationship between the person and the work. This would intercut nicely with the wide shot (at right).

The point-of-view (POV) shot

Similar to the shot/reverse shot is the classic—and sometimes cliché—point-of-view (or POV) shot. With this technique, you begin by shooting a person doing something, looking somewhere. And then (maybe at a later time) you shoot from your subject's position, so that we can see what the person was seeing. Here's a good example:

TIP: You may be tempted to use the POV for a moving shot: Someone is walking, and you want to simulate his view by shooting while you walk. You might put the camera at the height of your two-year-old—or of your dog—and "walk" through the house. You might point the camera at a highway or the trees passing above your head as you travel. This technique can work for a moment, but don't get carried away with these moving POV shots. (Follow the rules on moving the camera—that is, don't do it.)

As a special trick, it's good to know that a camera can "look" through another optical device. I have created many fun shots by putting the camcorder lens up to binoculars, telescopes, and even other cameras. It doesn't have the same result as looking through with your own eye, but if the secondary device is steady, you can get an interesting effect (particularly if you're shooting from the POV of the subject).

 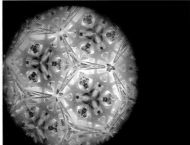

The cutaway shot (aka the insert)

A cutaway or *insert* is another special kind of shot. I might even go so far as to say that cutaways are my favorite shots. They're like little snapshots that provide texture and subtle detail; but most important for us now, they are images with no reference to real time. Let me explain.

When you edit, you need some shots that are completely unlinked—that can fit almost anywhere in your sequence. For instance, if you and I are talking on camera, I may need the camera to "look away" for a moment so that I can cut out some boring material. Almost anything will do for a cutaway: shots of a clock in the room, my foot bouncing nervously, books on the shelf, the cool shadow cast on a houseplant. I look at hands, at how the light is entering the room, or at any of the other odd little things around us.

TIP: Rule of thumb for cutaways: Make sure the shot does not include material of anyone talking—or, more precisely, of lips moving. A cutaway needs to work with no sound, or with sound of something else. One cutaway could simply be the shot of the person who is listening to the speaker—just looking or nodding, but not talking.

The top-down shot

Since it is easy to rotate the LCD display to face you even if the camera is pointed in some unusual direction, many situations can be covered with a sort of "top-down" approach—hold the camera out in front of you pointing down at a subject (such as kids sitting on the floor or eating a meal), rotate the LCD to face you, and shoot. It's a nice and sometimes-distinct vantage point that can give you more options in your editing. It's particularly nice for detail shots and cutaways.

The pickup

In a typical shooting situation, you will likely have shot the middle material first, then perhaps the ending, and finally the beginning, with the intention of rearranging the scenes when you edit. Even so, you may still have to go back a little (or a lot) later and shoot something you need to complete your coverage. This is what a pickup is. It's not a particular kind of shot—it's about your shooting process. Most of my pickups are cutaway shots; but as I mentioned earlier, I will sometimes fake a reverse shot of myself so that I can be in my own videos—technically speaking, these are pick ups, too. I don't need pickups all that often, but occasionally they can be lifesavers.

"Popping" between shots

In a perfect world, you'd shoot your close-up, stop recording, and then zoom out and take a wide shot. Then you'd stop recording again, move around for a reverse, frame it up neatly, brace yourself, and shoot some more...

Yeah, right—in your dreams.

In the real world, you will likely be shooting far more continuously, moving from wide shots to close shots, reframing, moving—all while you are still recording. My advice: At least *think* about each of these shots as distinct and discrete. The recorded moves, zooms, and pans that connect your shots are present for efficiency only. This material is largely unusable; don't mistake it for coverage.

Consequently, I try to make these transitional moments as short as possible. It means *popping* rapidly between close-ups and medium shots. No slow zooms here. I want to get to the next framed shot as quickly as possible. Because the action may last only a few seconds, I must make the most of each one of them—and not waste time moving slowly between shots. Popping increases the likelihood that my shots will cut together easily.

How long should a shot be?

Long enough. But not too long. *[Snicker.]*

But seriously, you should never record anything for less than a few seconds; I recommend 4. Even short 4-second shots may end up only 1 second long when they're edited. But that will happen later; for now, just make sure you get proper coverage. From the moment I press the Record button, I am generally trying to stay relaxed—important for keeping the camera steady—and using some discipline to hold still for the few seconds of the shot.

When you know you'll be editing the video, your shots can be pretty long (10 or 20 seconds is not uncommon) if you think first about what you're trying to accomplish. A long shot is probably either a series of *takes*—some kind of repetitive action happening over and over, and you're waiting for the right one—or maybe the documentary method of just shooting patiently until the action you're waiting for happens. The only problem with long shots is that you might be getting good material from this one vantage point while missing opportunities for necessary coverage from other positions. So balance your needs. Get at least two shots (a close-up and perhaps a medium shot) from the spot where you're standing, until you're pretty sure you have enough of both to edit. Then move on to the next position and do the same.

I rarely have shots that are exceptionally long, because once I've shot what I feel is enough material to edit, I want to move on to a new location and get a different angle (a reverse or maybe a wide shot). My desire to have at least three or four alternative versions of whatever I shoot prevents me from taking one long, boring shot.

Looking into the camera

Most rules of shooting and editing get squirrelly when a person is speaking and looking directly at the camera. It may be natural to talk to people while you're shooting and have them speak back to you, through the lens, but the material you get from these exchanges will not be easy to work with. Better (editing-wise) to hold the camera away from your face when you speak to someone on camera, so that she is looking at you and not the lens.

The Hollywood Way— a Helpful Paradigm

In the parlance of filmmaking, a setting for a particular part of the movie is called a *scene*. A scene is limited not by length but rather by location. A change of rooms is a change of scene; a change from inside to outside a building is usually a change of scene.

In Hollywood, scenes are labeled with a number that links them to a place in the script (as in "Scene 14"). Within each scene, the camera is set up in a single position and pointed in a certain direction, and the actors get in front of the lens and perform. Each shot taken from this one position is called a *setup*. For a single scene, there may be a bunch of setups: Wide shots and close-ups taken from the same physical location are still identified as different setups (as in "Scene 14A" and "Scene 14B," respectively). Therefore, a director covering a scene may shoot several setups from here, move the camera over there and shoot several more setups, and so on, until as quickly and inexpensively as possible, he's got the coverage he needs to complete this scene.

In truth, it doesn't take many setups to adequately cover a scene—far fewer than you might imagine. Some movie scenes are shot with a single setup; however, you really need at least two setups to be able to edit, and it is more common to have four to seven setups for any given scene (12 would be a lot). The words *scene* and *setup* are often used interchangeably (and setups are usually labeled with a scene number plus a suffix letter, as in "Scene 14A"), but they really denote different concepts.

To complicate matters even more, the actors perform "Scene 14A" on camera over and over until the director thinks he got it right. Each time they repeat the scene it is called a *take*. Thus, every setup requires at least one take, and often many.

Although for our purposes you won't have a tripod, actors, or a script (and no one is going to repeat performances for you over and over), the video you shoot can still best be described with terms like *scene, setup,* and *take.*

The little videos you are shooting will mostly be single scenes, or maybe small groups of scenes. Within each scene, you will be moving around to get different angles (the setups) and perhaps zooming in or out for even more setups. You don't want to "overcover" your scenes. A few key positions, each with a few different camera shots (which we'll get to soon), will be plenty to cover your scene professionally.

Watching the raw material

In Chapter 4 we will go over watching your video while organizing it (a process called *logging*). But usually, when you are pretty much done shooting your event, it is a good idea—and fun—to switch the camera to VCR mode, hit the Rewind button, and then play back your video. By watching your material immediately on the camera's LCD, you can quickly judge whether or not you've recorded the material you thought you had. If you are missing any elements, now is the time to do your pickups.

The most important part of watching this footage immediately is to get the tape to the last frame of video (and therefore of timecode) before you switch back to Camera mode. (Clearly, this is one of the disadvantages of tape-based cameras and a clear benefit of newer tapeless alternatives.) If you stop watching before the end of the video and then are suddenly called to action to shoot some more, you may inadvertently record over something good. This is a serious risk, and it can happen to anyone—even professionals. Switching your camera from Record to Play mode while you are still in a shooting situation must be done with care. And then there's the other extreme: If you slam your camera into fast-forward and overshoot the end of your recording (even by a little bit), you will land in no-timecode zone; and by recording more, you'll break your timecode.

Watching the video during the shooting process is fine, but the repercussions—accidentally taping over something you need, or breaking the timecode—are serious. You can be prepared for either situation by understanding timecode and knowing how to keep it continuous.

Assignment 6: Watch Some TV

Now that you are well versed in the lingua franca of video storytelling, let's watch some TV. (Oh, tell your parents I said it was OK.) I recommend an evening prime-time program, but not a sitcom, newscast, or music video. Not even a reality show. Just a plain old 60-minute

TV show, known in the business as *episodic programming.* Turn down the sound because it will distract you from the images and may also suck you into the narrative. Now, see if you can identify all the shots we've discussed. You'll notice various shots in almost any program, although they are often easiest to spot in a drama.

Do you see OS shots? Notice the inserts of hands, clocks, bombs—you name it—that break up the wider shots? Probably the coolest other thing to notice is really how few angles cover each scene. There may be many edits, but we keep returning to one of just a few setups: the shot of him, the shot of her, the shot of them both, and back to the shot of him.

Use the checklist below to see if you've spotted all the flora and fauna of a typical TV show:

- ▶ Interior shots (inside buildings)
- ▶ Exterior shots (outside buildings—you probably won't see too many of these)
- ▶ Establishing shots (could be in the credits or near commercial breaks, and they're likely motionless, exterior shots)
- ▶ Over-the-shoulder shots
- ▶ Close-up shots
- ▶ Medium shots (including two-shots)
- ▶ Wide shots
- ▶ Shot/reverse shots
- ▶ Cutaways
- ▶ Point-of-view shots

Takes and Repetition

Life is extremely repetitious. It also moves at a much slower pace than movies and television would lead us to believe. In the real world, we have long periods of silence and long moments when we are thinking, not doing. And then there are the moments when you are engaged in some activity that is itself highly repetitious in nature. You usually don't notice these things while they are happening, but when you remove yourself and watch—particularly while shooting a camera that is recording 30 snapshots every second—you will notice.

This repetition is what makes shooting editable video so easy. Repetition creates the equivalent of "takes," and you get to choose which takes will represent the action as a whole. In fact, the more repetitious something is, the easier it is to edit a video that represents it.

For example: If you are walking down a street, I can shoot you wide as you pass the park; then a minute or two later I can shoot a close-up of your feet stepping or your hands swinging or even the wind blowing your hair. And all of these shots will look natural when they're incorporated into the wider walking shot, primarily because of the repetitive nature of walking. Discontinuities will occur, for sure, but viewers tend not to notice these things as long as the action and emotion more or less match. (We'll discuss this further in Chapter 6.)

Framing and Design

Now that you are familiar with the elements of your video, you can start to think about how to make each shot as aesthetically appealing as possible. Even good coverage and snazzy editing cannot make up for poor focus and otherwise visually unattractive material. *Framing* is a general term for how the various objects and people you shoot are positioned in the horizontal rectangle of your video frame.

Most of the rules of good graphic design apply to video framing as well. You might even occasionally aspire to a video that if put in freeze-frame would make a fine photograph for your scrapbook. Here are some quick tips for better framing of your shots.

Centering (or, really, not centering)

Here's news: Whatever you're shooting (someone's head, for instance) doesn't always have to be in the center of each frame. There is nothing wrong with centering your subject; in fact, you will probably rely on this framing technique often. But, particularly with shots of people, it's nice if you can make a conscious choice between centering and not centering.

It's hard not to put the subject of a shot right in the center of every frame. It's a constant battle. If you don't put something in the center—particularly with cameras that are set to auto-focus or automatic exposure—you may have problems getting it in focus or even properly exposed. (Of course, this is a good reason to learn more about your camera's manual controls, but that's another story.) But even with auto-everything, you can still frame shots nicely even if you don't center them. Get used to looking around the frame and determining if the space around your subject appears appropriate. Sometimes this will mean placing the subject in the center, and sometimes it won't.

Balance

Take some advice from magazine and book designers: They don't want every picture on a page to be the same size. To get something noticed, to add emphasis, they make some larger. Pictures on the page of a book are analogous to the various objects in your frames of video: Balance the objects in the frame—a big one here, lots of little things over there; something in the foreground here, something in the background over there (see **Figure 3.5**).

FIGURE 3.5 Here are a couple of hypothetical book pages. When every object is the same size, the page is pretty dull—it has no focus, no main event. It looks like a page from a yearbook. On the other hand, when you play with the relative sizes of the page objects, the same images in a different layout get some pizzazz. It's not hard to do, but it won't happen on its own.

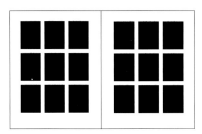 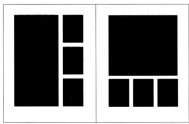

Perhaps it's too much to ask that you not only keep your timecode continuous (as we discussed earlier) but also make each shot beautiful and well framed. But good framing is not all that hard to do. Because you are not moving while you shoot, you can easily take a moment to frame the scene through the viewfinder (or LCD) in a nice way. I will keep my tips on framing to a bare minimum. Remember these two things:

▸ **The Rule of Thirds:** The subject does not always have to be in the middle of your frame. In fact, it usually should *not* be exactly in the middle. Generally, you want your subject about one-third of the way into the frame, either on the left or right, top or bottom.

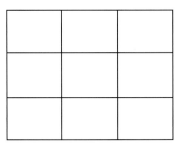 

▶ **Looking *into* the Frame:** It usually looks better when the extra space in your frame (created when you're following the Rule of Thirds) is *in front of* the subject being framed. The subject should move or look *into* that space.

Both of these rules are somewhat easier to manage within the cinematic 16:9 (wide-screen) format because the increased width makes it clearer when the subject is placed on a one-third point. Also, a squarer canvas can be rather dull visually, whereas a wide-screen simply gives you more space to play with in terms of composition and balance.

Safe frame margins

Just as with printed pages, video also requires margins for both creative and technical reasons.

It is difficult to know how a video will play on different displays, and consumer television sets are even designed to cut off the edges of frames when videos play. To be safe, you need to know where the margins are. Within each frame is a region where you can be sure that viewers will see what you've shot. Around that region is a kind of gray zone that may or may not get cropped by your TV, and then there is the outside edge of the frame, which you can be reasonably certain will not be seen on TV monitors, even though you will see it in the camera and on your computer. The two zones of safety, known as *title safe* and *action safe*, are defined this way:

Editing software sometimes allows you to superimpose safe margin lines while you work. This feature is helpful for titles and effects, but it comes too late in the process to save video that is shot without regard for the margins.

Just remember that not every bit of video you shoot will end up on your TV monitor. Use your imagination to try blocking out those outside elements as you compose shots.

Title safe: The innermost region, where the content is perfectly safe on pretty much any monitor. This margin is the limit for text and titles if you want guaranteed readability.

Action safe: The outer safety margin, outside of which the viewer likely won't see the material that you recorded onto the frame.

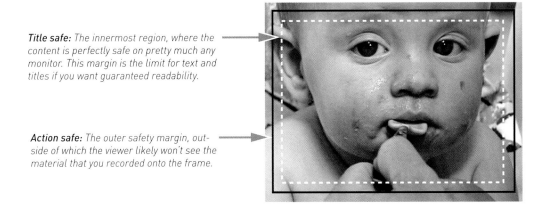

Stop Moving the Camera

If you get nothing else from this book, get this:

Stand still. Stop moving yourself or the camera around!

Professionals get to move the camera for a handful of reasons:

- ▶ They have many people and specially designed equipment that allows them to move the camera steadily, smoothly, and at the appropriate focus.

- ▶ They have a lot of time to set up each shot.

- ▶ They get to rehearse moves with the camera operator, the focuser, and the actors.

- ▶ They get multiple tries to get it right.

Unless you have at least one of these four factors on your side (and preferably more), keep the camera still. This takes practice and conviction, and may at first seem impossible. But you'll soon find that it is easier to stay still than to move around. Entire movies have been shot with little or no camera movement. You can do it, too.

Assignment 7: At the Dog Park

This assignment is designed to emphasize a couple of valuable points about moving your camera. I hope that it will help you learn some good shooting habits.

You probably have a park near your house where all the dogs go to play, right? Good. Take yourself and your camera (and your dog, if you have one) to this park. Sit down on a bench.

Now pick out a dog—one that is particularly appealing and jovial—and shoot only this dog for the next 60 seconds.

Rewind the tape and watch your video.

Do you like what you see? Or does watching it make you queasy? If the dog you shot is like my dog, he was in constant motion, and you were moving around trying to follow him. This makes for a video that's hard to watch.

If you were in a close-up mode, the picture may be bouncing all over, losing your canine subject and then finding him again as you pan around looking for him. If you were in a wide-shot mode, you probably panned around a little less but always tried to keep the dog in the middle of the frame.

This kind of material can make you feel nauseated if you watch it for any length of time. The background is blurry; the dog is bouncing in and out of frame.

NOTE: There is a subtle but important difference between moving the camera to look around at things (called *panning*) and moving the camera to keep a moving subject in the frame (called *tracking*). Panning, which is technically a side-to-side motion, and its evil twin, *tilting* (an up-and-down motion), are best left to professionals equipped with special tripods. Tracking can be done pretty well with a camcorder, but the key is not to overuse it; even too much tracking can be hard to watch.

Although this graphic example of the perils of moving your camera may leave you a bit discouraged, don't worry—and don't resign yourself to shooting still-life arrangements forever. Motion is an essential ingredient in video, and it can work for you. Make it your servant.

How not to move the camera

I developed some tricks to help me stop moving the camera when my subjects are in motion. Any or all of the following tips will help you keep your shots "static":

▶ Practice bracing against something, or look at the background of the frame and identify some landmarks you want to hang on to. You may drift a little, but we're not worried about drift.

▶ Practice moving your eye around the frame instead of moving the frame around the subject. The screen is your canvas, and the object in motion is simply moving around the canvas. And remember that subjects do not need to be in the middle of the frame; it isn't that hard to keep a frame somewhere around the subject.

▶ Remember that subjects are free to enter into and exit out of your frame. This is important. They don't need to start or end in-frame. I usually begin with my subjects off to one side of the frame (remember the Rule of Thirds), moving into the blank part of the frame (remember to let your subject face into the frame), so that if they move out of the frame, at least I will have had them onscreen for the maximum time.

Shoot a little wide. If you shoot close-up, the subject can exit the frame with very little movement. This can be frustrating. But if you do a medium shot or go wide, the subject has enough room that the frame can accommodate some motion without your having to move the camera.

Assignment 8: More Dog Park

OK, now let's shoot some dog video again. Sit back down on the park bench, get comfortable, find the dog, hold still, zoom out a bit more... Now record! Let the dog run into the frame; then watch him run out of it. Stop recording and look at where he's heading. Aim the camera ahead of him, stop, hold still, and shoot some more. Again, let the dog run into and out of the frame. If you get lucky, he may stop right in the frame, do something cool, and then leave. Shoot for another minute or two.

Watch your new dog video and compare it with the first one (see **Figure 3.6**). Easier to watch?

FIGURE 3.6 It takes great discipline to hold a camera still while shooting something that is moving. You have to break your old camera habits and develop new ones. Although it's hard to tell with a still image, the shot on the left is framed around the dogs and lets them subsequently run out of the frame. The shot on the right is wider, so even though the dogs are running around, it's easier to stay still.

In the first assignment, you probably had just one long mess of video containing some good parts tracking your dog, as well as some bad parts where you are whipping around looking for him, zooming in and out, and so on. The second assignment should illustrate to you how much discipline it takes *not* to track a moving object. What you need when you get to the editing phase is really *both* kinds of shots. Mostly you'll want the static shots, but the occasional (short) good tracking bit can be useful, too. The only way you'll get both is to learn to stop tracking at will.

Moving the camera

Let's be realistic: Try as you might, it is practically impossible never to move while shooting. With this in mind, consider the following points.

First, think of a moving shot as a *special effect*. Like all special effects, moving shots can add to your story, but they aren't the story itself. Second, you never *have* to move the camera to get a shot. There is virtually no shot that you can get by moving the camera that can't be skillfully done (even by a beginner) using a small series of static shots. Moving around has its place, but the risks do often outweigh the rewards.

Remember that when a camera moves, it shakes and bounces the image around. Image-stabilization technology (a feature of most digital camcorders—see the sidebar coming up) can definitely help, but it can't fix everything: If the camera bounces too much, the shots will still be unwatchable. If you could always move slowly and smoothly as you shot, this wouldn't be a problem. But to move slowly and smoothly all the time, you'd need special equipment.

If you must move the camera (and every one of you will insist that you must), make moves that are *very small and very controlled*. What feels like a tiny, insignificant movement is likely all that will be required for the shot.

These are my personal rules for moving the camera:

1. If I want to track a moving object, I do it. But I don't waste a lot of time with this material, and I always get myself a static (and usually wider) shot of the same object.

2. If possible, I practice the move before I shoot. If it's a small move, I perform it a couple of times while recording.

3. If I am tracking an object in motion, at some point I stop moving, hold the camera still, and let the object exit the frame.

4. While I don't measure these things precisely, my guess is that my moves are smaller than 15 degrees of arc. I never do a panorama of a horizon or a long 90- to 180-degree vista. That's simply too much.

5. I hold the camera as close as I can to my face and pull my elbows tight against my sides. I use both hands to hold the camera body. I pivot from my waist.

Even following all my own rules, I can only rarely pull off a nice move. If I couldn't slow down these shots with the computer while editing, I'd probably never be able to use them. Luckily, there is *some* hope of saving them in post-production. (More on that when we get to editing, in Chapter 6.)

Image Stabilization

A technology built into many camcorders, image stabilization uses either optical or digital means to accommodate tiny movements of your camera (and consequently your video). While image stabilization slightly decreases the resolution of your video to accomplish this goal, most reviewers report that the benefits are real and worthwhile. But image stabilization will not solve all problems, particularly when the movement is extreme. It works best cleaning up the most common type of camera movement—the movement that results from trying to hold the camera *still*. It won't help much with, say, a wild pan.

Lighting

Although I insisted earlier that you use only existing lighting, this doesn't mean that you should ignore lighting altogether or aren't allowed to play with it. Light is the paint of photography. You need it very much. If a scene is fully lit, you'll probably be happy with it. But what if it's not?

Dark scenes

Dimly lit scenes pose a few challenges. To get enough light into the camera in the dark location, the camera (in automatic-exposure mode) will open up as much as it can, letting more light through the aperture behind the lens. If you can't collect enough light this way, the only other option is to expose the frame for a longer time by slowing down the shutter speed. This is easy to do manually—but you may want to skip it unless you're already comfortable switching your camera from automatic to manual control.

When the shutter speed drops below 1/30 of a second, some interesting visual effects will occur (see **Figure 3.7**). On the one hand, these effects are "natural" properties of the light and the camera, as opposed to "digital" computer-generated effects. On the other hand, the resulting video won't look much like real life: The frames will be a little blurry, and the overall look will be jumpy, staccato, and somewhat like an old-fashioned movie.

FIGURE 3.7 When the shutter speed gets slow, video gets *weird*.

Many people don't like this look, but I do. To me, the blur and jumpiness add to the mystery of photography done in the dark. When everything is shrouded in darkness, it feels more appropriate to approximate what is going on. Yes, the video can be hard to watch. Any camera motion is more noticeable—and potentially more irritating—to the viewer. When you go into a situation of low light and a slow shutter speed, your best bet is to hold very still or, better yet, prop the camera up on something solid while you shoot.

Autofocus is deeply troubled in the dark. It will move in and out of focus trying to "see" what you are looking at. It's no better for you to take the camera out of autofocus and grab the controls yourself, so I don't recommend doing this either. Just keep the camera still and, at least for today, treat this focus drift as an "effect" of your low-light shoot.

NOTE: These lighting and motion effects are surreal, that is true. But consider this: They are to regular video what black-and-white is to color photography. All video and photography is only a partial representation of our perception of reality. By experimenting with these motion effects, perhaps you can better reveal other aspects— excitement, mystery—of the video.

Backlighting

The most common lighting challenges facing video folks are those where a lot of light is behind your subject. In general, you should shoot with your back to the light, rather than shooting into it. But this isn't always possible. And it might come up when you're trying to get a reverse shot.

On automatic exposure, your camera will try to handle the backlit situation. But it can't, and your subject will be cloaked in darkness, like a silhouette—probably not the result you were hoping for. You

can usually move either yourself or the camera to correct the problem. Of course, backlit scenes are only a problem if you *don't* want that cool-looking silhouetted shot. Remember, not every shot you take must be front-lit, evenly illuminated, and all in focus; it is perfectly fine to have dark shots and other interesting, moody frames in your project. And if the shots don't work, you can always edit them out later. This is all part of learning how to see things differently with a camera in your hand.

If you don't like this at all, your camera must be switched from auto to manual exposure, and you need to compensate for the odd lighting. Many cameras have a feature called *back light*, which instantly corrects for most backlighting situations by overexposing the shot. Even without switching from auto, you can force the camera to temporarily adjust exposure and improve the image.

Sound Coverage

It's important to think of sound as its own entity, like video, and not as an essential component of video. You can look at images with no sound (snapshots, silent movies), and you can listen to sound with no images (radio, CDs). Keep this in mind when you watch your video: You are actually doing two things at the same time—seeing the video and listening to the audio recorded with it.

Consequently, when we discuss coverage, there are two kinds: There is sound coverage you need to get, as well as the video coverage we described above. The first (and most obvious) sound you need is the synchronous, or *sync*, sound that goes along with the video you've been shooting.

Picture and sound are separate entities and must be synchronized with each other for it to look like words are coming out of your mouth. Of course, your camera does this automatically, but did you know that professional movie cameras in Hollywood don't? They just shoot pictures, and an entirely separate group of people (and equipment) record the sound at the same time. It has to be synchronized by hand, and kept in sync whenever picture or sound is edited.

So sync sound is the first kind of sound coverage you need. The other kinds of coverage are sounds that you record with your camera without concerning yourself (much) with the images that your camera automatically records in the process. Here are the key types of sound coverage.

Ambience

I have a trick for getting good audio in my videos: I get some ambient sounds to work with.

Ambience is the background sound of a scene. At the beach, it is the sound of the ocean waves. At a bar or pub, it is the din of crowds and bottles and music. Even in the quietest places, there is some kind of ambient sound—even if it's just the sound of silence. (This is sometimes called *room tone*.)

If you have time after you've shot your first main shot or series of shots, take one more—a 30- to 60-second shot without stopping. Listen carefully while you record. You don't want this material for the picture; you want it for the sound—and you may need it when editing to help create a seamless stream of audio that you can use for background sounds. It won't sync to anything, but it's real, and it's called *location sound* (or sometimes *fill*).

I've found a few scenarios where having ambience is particularly useful:

▸ **When I'm shooting somewhere that's windy.** On windy days, many of my shots end up containing a lot of loud "wind noise." Depending on which way I'm facing (toward the wind or downwind), this noise will vary greatly. Ambience in this situation would mean finding a spot where there is no wind (perhaps a protected cove) and where I can hear the *actual* sounds of the place—birds, the ocean, a light breeze in the trees. When I go to edit, I will use this clean ambience for the sound track, instead of all the wind-noise audio.

▶ **When I'm at a party.** Parties produce very unique and consistent ranges of noise—mixtures of many conversations, dishes clanking, and often music. When you listen to the ambience of a party, you can be looking simultaneously at almost any images from the party, and the sound and video will fit together well. This is a very useful trick to keep in mind.

▶ **When I'm anywhere that music is playing.** If I want to use real-world music as part of a video I'll be editing, I must record with the music completely unbroken—which means I can't turn the camera off and on. Whether it's people dancing to a song or someone singing on a stage, I'll need a separate recording of the music itself, with no interruptions.

▶ **When I'm anywhere the ambience is interesting.** At the beach, the zoo, a racetrack, a football game—each place has a distinct ambient sound, and I might find it useful later to have a long, clean recording of just that sound.

Don't worry about dialog

This statement may raise some eyebrows. After all, how do you get sync sound but no dialog? My point here is only this: You will get production sound, dialog, and all that other audio stuff without even trying. And you will be listening to people talking all the time while you shoot. But to use dialog effectively in your videos requires editing skills that I think are a little too advanced for our purposes here. In our shoot, just understand that recording conversations may not produce the results you are hoping for. Eventually, as your video skills (and maybe your software tools) get more advanced, you can use dialog in many ways. For now, though, don't think about it.

Besides, the oldest rule in Hollywood applies here: *Show it, don't tell it.* If you want to make a strong point, use action rather than dialog.

Turn off the music when you shoot

Like special effects, music is best if added later, when you can better control it. If you want a video that has music playing in it, the best thing to do is shoot a video without the music playing. If you've recorded music in the background while people are simultaneously talking, it will all end up mixed together in your audio track; you won't be able to edit the talking without affecting the music. Handling this situation is almost impossible and quite discouraging. You can't edit out a line of conversation without creating a distracting jump in the music. Similarly, there would be no way to remove only the music (and replace it with a song from a CD, for instance) and still have any of the talking intact.

You may find yourself at a party, in a car, or at a special event where music plays in the background while you want to shoot people talking and having fun. You may not be able to turn down the music (remember that you should interfere in a scene as little as possible), so be aware that recording it may limit your editing options later on.

What to Shoot: Small Moments

Remembering to shoot big events is easy. After all, they are what most camcorders are used for—weddings, birthdays, Christmas morning, your child's first steps, a school play, bringing home your new car.

Big events are, by definition, important events. When you don't shoot often, I suppose it's fine to get the big events. **But don't forget the small moments.** Capturing them will be the best thing you ever do with your camcorder.

It is the small moments that will make for great videos that may even be more cherished than big events as time goes by. Small moments are too easily forgotten, but they are the true fabric of our lives. Small moments are somewhat random; they are happening all around us all the time. Here are some of my favorite personal examples:

- A typical mealtime in your home
- Your workday
- Your commute (but don't drive while you shoot!)
- Your messy bedroom (what *are* all those things in that pile?)
- The items on your bedside table
- The walking of your dog (including your dog's point of view)
- A visit to the playground with your kid
- Holiday cookies being baked for neighborhood gifts
- A rainy day at home
- The late-night sounds and midnight shadows inside your house
- The preparation for any big event (wedding, play) but not the event itself.
- Your baby waking up in the morning

There is no "point" to recording these everyday occurrences, other than to capture a moment in time—one of the things that video does best. When I watch other people's videos, I can appreciate the shots of their kids, but I love seeing how other people live and how they see it themselves. When I watch old archival footage of Hollywood or New York City, my favorite parts are the details of people's daily lives. It's fine to see wide shots of them running around on the city streets, and close-ups of their faces, but I prefer seeing them shopping in a grocery store (look at those funky old brands!) or loading stuff into the car's trunk (I've never seen that model of automobile before!).

Unlike software, your videos should be a little "dated," filled with shots that couldn't be from just anywhere or anytime, but rather are uniquely you in a unique place in time. Images of technological devices like phones, stereos, and computers show our place in time rather well (because they change so often), as do the sounds and images of popular culture, including Top 40 radio tunes, TV shows, newspapers, magazines, and clothing fashion. All these are nice for insert shots into your video sketches.

The expense of small moments

My neighbor Steve told me that sometimes he wants to shoot a small moment, but then he thinks that maybe the camera is too special or the tape too expensive to "waste" on something that is not "important." My only response is that the biggest expense is now behind you, and not using the equipment would be the biggest waste.

NOTE: For tapeless camcorders, make sure you calculate in the cost of the media. For HDD, you'll need a significant quantity of hard disk storage available to your computer; for memory stick-type cameras, the multi-GB little storage devices can cost hundreds of dollars.

Also, a camcorder's only real operating expense is the cost of videotape. At less than $4 per 60-minute tape, video is inexpensive for what you get, I think, though the cost is not inconsequential. But that's just me; you will need to set a video budget and assess your financial commitment to this medium.

Finally, I think the biggest expense of DV is not the money itself, but rather the way it coaxes you out of a situation so that you can shoot it. I can be having a special moment with my friends and suddenly think to myself, "I wish I had my camera here now," but I don't want to stop the moment to go get it. Leaving to find the camera, readying the tape… that can be a drag. It may take a few minutes to prep, and the camera itself may change the situation when you return. You must find your personal balance here. I don't suggest recording every small moment, but periodically I do drag out my camera in these situations. About half the time I'm thrilled that I did.

The other half of the time, the moment ends when I leave (or when I return with a lens). My method for minimizing this last drawback is to keep the camera ready as much as I can. When I'm done using it, I always set it back up so that it's ready to go the next time: tape in place with safety off and cued to the last frame of video (and thus of timecode) and battery charged up.

Candid photography

Everyone knows that candid shots are special and often make for better video, but for some reason most people have trouble shooting them.

When a camera comes out, the photographer will invariably line up all the subjects and announce, "OK, everyone, look over here and say 'Cheese'!" Catching people just being themselves and being natural is a wonderful skill to have.

In these images, you can see me shooting a sketch one Halloween. Not only can you see typical camera/body positions, but you can generally see how I keep out of the way of the action and just shoot from off to the side.

VIDEO ONLINE: Have a look at Sketch C, http://ldvb.blogspot.com

Unfortunately for you, many people think of using a hidden camera more like spying than photojournalism. A good rule of thumb is to make sure any group knows that you're slinking around with a camera and that you probably won't be cluing them in on when you're shooting and when you're just looking around. (I turn off the red light and disable the camera beep; although it is more honest to keep them on, they can be quite distracting to people and consequently alter your "candid" mode.)

I could go on for a separate book about the issues and ethics associated with videography. The most important thing for you now is to understand that shooting video of people can be threatening, and you need to be clear with your subjects that you will be recording them. If they trust you, there may be no problem. But if they don't want to be shot, it's best to take them at their word.

Non-candid photography

Here's another shooting style that is common to home video: Put the camera in people's faces, talk to them and interview them, and let them address you through the camera lens directly. This produces

material totally unlike all the coverage we've discussed in this chapter. And while fun and interesting, shooting this way can produce video that can be difficult to edit into the other coverage. You can be non-candid, interview people, and still get material that is easy to edit, but it requires keeping your head out from behind the camera. Hold the camera at your side or lower down (chest height) pointing up, and have them talk to your face, not your camera. I've even interviewed friends with the camera in my hand, held high above my head pointing down. You might feel a little weird doing it, but if you can forget about the camera, they may, too, and the video can be pretty cool.

Particle Physics and DV

In 1920s Werner Heisenberg described something that applies both to particle physics and, apparently, to home video: More accurately known as the "Observer Effect," it is well known that the act of watching something changes the event being observed. In other words, you can't ever be perfectly candid. When people know you have a camera, they will behave differently. (I know that my kids did this when they were little. They would see the lens and stop whatever they were doing to investigate.) Adults are more subtle.

If you want truly candid photography, do what you can to keep yourself and your camera inconspicuous. Shoot wide, and shoot from far away before you get closer—just in case whatever you want to capture radically changes or ends when you show up.

On the left is some video I shot of my son; he's talking directly to me, and I'm stationed behind the lens. It's usually harder to work this into a video sketch, but it's interesting and fun raw footage. On the right is an interview I did with my daughter before Mother's Day. She too is looking toward me, but I'm to the side of the camera, so she isn't staring at the lens. A subtle but significant difference. Another good angle can be achieved by holding the camera low in front of yourself and to the side.

The truth is that the camera *is* a part of the scene and event, and even candid photography is often only an approximation of people acting natural (as if no camera were present). Sometimes it's better to just be out with it, let people be completely aware you are there to video them, and start shooting. But I think it's best to keep expectations low with non-candid material.

How Often to Shoot

This is perhaps the hardest question for someone new to video. In particular because you probably also have a digital still camera of some kind, and now every time you go out you're wondering if you have to lug your camcorder, your digital SLR, and cell phone, and it's a pain. To that I can only relay what I've found: Don't shoot everything. Most days I am not interested in shooting. Then on other days I just make a decision that I'm going to carry a camera of some kind around for a bit and see what I see.

But just because you've decided to carry the videocamera out today, whether you're walking your dog or going to your kid's soccer game, it doesn't mean you're going to find anything you really want to shoot. And if you do, you must remember your job on that day: *Shoot no more than 20 minutes of video*. It will be hard.

Think about it: You want to shoot at the soccer game. You're not a sports journalist. You have a limited vantage point, (and besides, you'd like to watch the game and cheer). You can't (or shouldn't) shoot 90 minutes of video. You need to pick ONE quarter, and decide to shoot it, and your mantra is that you're not videoing *this game*, but you're using this game to represent the *games* of soccer you have been attending this season. So you don't just shoot the action, but you also shoot the spectators. You chronicle the gearing up in a couple quick shots. The drive maybe, if it's strikes you. The snacks. The little kids running around the sidelines. Everything. You gather up all the bits and you make a video about soccer. This is very different from documenting the entire game (and every game) of the season.

Summary

Think of using a camcorder as a scaled-up version of taking pictures with your regular old still camera, rather than as a scaled-down version of making theatrical feature films. Boring photographic rules like framing and exposure still apply for shooting good-looking video material. This chapter introduced you to the kinds of video you should be trying to capture—the elements you will need later when you go to edit. Ultimately, your finished videos will only be as good as the raw footage you shoot.

Organizing Your Video

Organizing your videotapes is so important that it's really too bad it seems rather boring and tedious. It's certainly not as glamorous as shooting, and it's even more clerical than editing. Nevertheless, organizing is key. You may never edit all your tapes, but every one of them should be organized. One of the secrets to editing well is knowing what material you have to work with, and the only way you will know this is if you've watched all of your tapes at least once. It's only natural to take some notes as you watch a tape, and this chapter will guide you in how to label tapes, take notes efficiently, and prepare for editing should you decide that's what you want to do.

One of the biggest drawbacks to tapeless camcorders is the serious challenge associated with organizing, storing, and logging your video. Because tapeless alternatives pose their own series of workflows, I will deal only with tape-based video here, and save insights in the ever-changing future for my online blog (http://ldvb.blogspot.com).

What's great about organizing your material is that even if you choose not to edit, you will *really* know what is on each of your videotapes. Sometimes years after shooting something, for example, I might be working on an unrelated project when I decide I need a certain kind of shot (a sunset, my parents on vacation, a plane landing at an airport) to fill in a hole or take advantage of an opportunity I created while editing. Through clear and simple organization, I am my own hero in these situations—and you can be one, too. Take a few easy steps to keep your video organized.

Organizing Your Materials

Most of my friends, when they first start shooting video, end up with stacks of unlabeled tapes scattered next to their computers. While it may not be a big problem at first, disorganization can grow into a nightmare.

I was at my friend Hilary's house recently, about a month after she began her personal adventure with digital video, and I asked to see her editing setup. I looked over her Mac, and she showed me some videos she had cut. She also had a small pile of DV tapes on the desk. None were labeled.

"Why didn't you label your tapes?" I asked.

"Well," she replied, "I never imagined I'd have more than a few... I thought I knew what was on them."

Hilary's assumption is a common one, but it can be a big mistake. Here is the typically erroneous logic behind it:

▶ I'm just starting out, so labeling seems too fastidious. (Like alphabetizing your CD collection, or worse, arranging your socks.)

▶ I'm just starting out and have only two or three tapes, so why bother?

▶ I know what's on my tapes, since I shot them and watched them myself.

▶ Organizing is for geeks. I'm far too hip to care.

But here's the truth: You are eventually going to have more tapes than you have today; you will forget what is on each tape in short order; and organizing (geeky though it may be) is the cornerstone to good filmmaking or even just personal enjoyment of your videos. So get used to it. Make it a habit. Here's how.

Labeling the tape

Back in Chapter 2 I urged you to put a label referencing the date, like "S08.12.24," on your first videotape. I hope you heeded this advice. Here's a little more detail on the organizational process.

When you unpack a new videotape, do the following:

1.   Take the paper stuff out of the box.

2.   Label the top and long side of the tape (there's a groove there for a label; see **Figure 4.1**).

3.   Throw out all the paper things you just pulled out of the box.

Easy, isn't it? Now that you have a routine for labeling every new cassette, let's get into the details about finding material on your tapes.

NOTE: There is not one way to organize. There are many. But determining what is right for you often involves a period of trial and error. The method I'm encouraging you to use has evolved from my original simpler method, which wasn't holding up to the test of time. I've been using this improved method for a few years now and it works nicely for me, and I think it will work for you. If you choose to develop your own way, more power to you. I happen to think this method is pretty good, though.

FIGURE 4.1 It doesn't matter whether you fill out your labels and then attach them to the tape, or attach them first and then fill them out. Just make it easy for yourself and keep your labeling simple and clear. Consistent is nice, too.

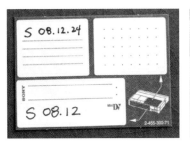 

Tape labels: "Reel names"

In professional circles, each tape is known as a *reel*. In all but the most basic editing systems, when a tape is in a camera that is connected to a computer, the software that deals with videotapes will ask you which reel you are now watching and editing. You must label your tapes with reel names—or, in our case, reel numbers.

While there is nothing inherently wrong with writing descriptive names on the labels that come with each videotape, it isn't a particularly good way to label (or locate) your material. Neither is filling out the white cover sheet that lines the cassette box. This is one reason I throw this stuff out. So even though I do have tapes with labels like "Trip to NYC" or "Alina's Birthday," I devised a simple naming and numbering system to keep track of all my tapes. I use a boring alphanumeric code: a letter designating what type of tape it is, and a number—it's simple, it's clean, and it keeps tapes relatively orderly.

The letter code can be based on whatever is important to you. I suggest the following:

- ► *S* **for "Source":** A tape containing the original source material shot with your digital video camcorder, unedited and raw. (It could also stand for "Shooting," if that's easier to remember.)

▶ *M* **for "Master":** A tape dedicated to recordings of your finished edited sequences. Don't put your edited footage back on the source tapes. It's good to keep cut material separated from raw.

▶ *A* **for "Analog":** I have lots of material on old analog VHS, S-VHS, and Hi-8 tapes that I want to convert to the digital format for long-term storage, logging, and editing. I dub the old tapes to DV and code the new DV tape to easily differentiate it from video that originated out of a digital camera.

▶ *C* **for "Culled":** Not frequently, but on occasion, I will dump an entire S tape into the computer, and spend a rapid hour or two culling it down to 20–30 minutes. You'll hear about this in Chapter 5, but culling is not editing in that all you're doing is making a raw tape more watchable by deleting bad, long, or unwatchable video segments. Once culled, I dump the entire tape back onto another tape, a "C" tape with the same name.

If these letter codes don't work for you, make up your own. A couple of suggestions, though: Don't create a code system based on *content* (*B* for "Baby" or *H* for "House" or *V* for "Vacation"), because your raw footage may fall into many different categories. And don't use "names" for your tapes. Forget "Las Vegas," "Boat Launching," or "Summer 2009." The problem with names isn't one of description—they may well describe precisely what is *on* each tape— but rather one of organization. If you go by names, you could have filed that footage from your weekend in Las Vegas under "Las" or "Vegas" or even "weekend."

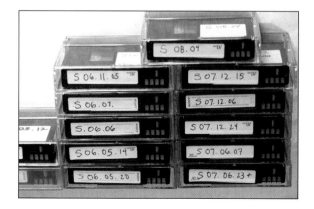

On the other hand, it's easy to put your sources tapes in order when they're labeled with year/month. Anyway, a consistent numbering system makes your tapes easy to identify, free from many problems of handwriting legibility, and simple to identify and organize.

For naming master tapes I use an even simpler method: I use an "M" followed by a number—just an ordinary sequential number. (I started at 1 and I'm up to 25 today.)

Consequently, it's really easy to know where to find tape M4 (hint: It's stacked between M3 and M5), and this is particularly important, since these tapes contain many different videos covering any kind of time range. Master tapes have no place in time, so I've found it's best just to number them in order.

"S09.3" or "M4" may not be a fun or descriptive name for a tape, but we can rely on log sheets for content description. And the name combined with a logging process really makes this system work. By glancing at my log sheets, I know for a fact that the best sunset shot I have ever recorded is about 45 minutes into tape S05.12—a tape that, under a different labeling system, would probably be called "Garden Project." So stick with simple codes on your tapes, and if you must add text to the label, add it after the number. (Less than 5 percent of my tapes demand any kind of special notation.)

Tape labels: Minimalist descriptions

After using only reel names for about five years, I began to need a little bit more info on the tapes. Yes, I kept a log book, but more often than not, I found myself grabbing a tape to watch and having *no* idea what was on it. While this doesn't replace a bona fide log book, I now believe that writing a description on the tape label is helpful. This is what I write:

1. **Date I put the tape in the camera.** Since I don't remove tapes until they are full (or almost full), a tape generally has start and end dates associated with it. I can put the start date on when I'm adding the label, and I add the end date when I remove it—both of which happen even before I sit down to log.

2. **Teeny tiny description of what events are on the tape.** This is also not to be confused with logging. But if there is a general theme to the *entire* tape, or a big part of the tape, I've found it useful to add it here. Stuff like "Jonah's Birthday" or "Boat Trip" or "Family Interviews." The danger is that you don't log the tape, and think this covers it—which it usually won't. But the converse is also a danger, that you don't have any log *and* no description, and you forget quickly which of the three tapes sitting here is the one from the party. I have many (most) tapes without this additional info; but by all means, feel free to add it if that helps.

Logging

You can't edit your videotapes if you don't know what's on them. The key to finding out what's on them is to (1) shoot with continuous timecode, (2) label your tapes, and (3) log your tapes. We've already discussed keeping your timecode "clean" (go back to Chapter 2 if you need a refresher), and we've already covered proper labeling methods. Now it's time to watch and log your tapes.

The purpose of a log is to help you find shots you want to use later. One of the most brutally boring tasks in "old-fashioned" editing is having to shuttle through miles of film or tape just to find the bits that are good. Computers make this chore simpler, but only if you have a log. It is a critical part of your setup. All the fancy computer and camera equipment in the world can't replace a good log book.

NOTE: The term *dailies* refers to the raw footage taken the previous day. In Hollywood, film is shot during the day, goes to the processing lab that evening, is printed, and is picked up the next morning. Then, once a day—usually the day after being shot—the film is watched. Because it happens every day, it is called *dailies*. Some films, in particular those with odd shooting schedules, instead have *nightlies*.

Logging your DV tapes can be tedious. If you fall behind in the process and your tapes are stacking up, you run the risk of not doing it at all. Don't let that happen. Make logging a game. In Hollywood, "screening the dailies" is a time-honored tradition. The director, cinematographer, editor, and actors all get together for an hour or so to watch the material that was shot. This is when they make notes about what is good and what is not, which shots must be used, and how the project might come together. It's fun, like a little party.

While it is fun to shoot, keep the footage hidden, and then emerge from your editing retreat and surprise your family with a neat finished video, it can be just as entertaining to show the raw footage to everyone *in* the video. Watch dailies with your family, get their input, and create a log together. Many people actually want to see the raw video to catch all the special moments, but I think it's good to announce up front that unedited material is *supposed* to be boring and long, even for cool movies in Hollywood.

A simple tape log will contain the reel name and a list of shot descriptions and timecode references. Timecode, for our purposes here, is just a counter. It starts at 0 at the beginning of the tape and runs unbroken until the tape ends (generally about 1 hour). If you keep it continuous and unbroken, and the camera is working properly, the timecode is the perfect reference number for a bit of video. Professional timecode numbers look complicated because they are so long (usually eight digits). You should abbreviate your logged timecodes to just *minutes* and *seconds*—for example, *2:36* would be read as "2 minutes, 36 seconds." (Listing *hours* probably won't be necessary most of the time for 1-hour tapes, because generally they run only about 3 minutes over an hour.)

If you still have problems reading or writing timecode, go back to Chapter 2 for more complete coverage of the topic.

Now that you can read and write timecode, you can log your tape. First, make sure the right tape is in your camera. Then turn on the timecode display. Different cameras do this in slightly different ways, but usually you look for a button marked Display. Like the date and time a shot was recorded, the timecode is always captured when you shoot, but it need not be displayed. I like to *edit* with timecode turned off, but you must *log* with timecode turned on (see **Figure 4.2**).

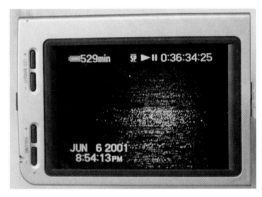

FIGURE 4.2 One of the first things I do when logging (or even just watching) a video-tape is turn on the timecode, shown here at the top right of the LCD. Sometimes I turn on the data code on the bottom so that I can see the date, but only if this tape covers a lot of dates.

Tape logs

Once your tapes are labeled with a simple and clear numbering system, you are ready to log them. Use one clean sheet of paper per tape, with the tape's reel name at the top and timecodes, dates, and descriptions making up the body of the log.

TAPE # S.O.1.O4

DV LOGSHEET

start time	end time	date	description
OO:OO		4/23/01	Jonah on floor
4:10			Jen paints toes
6:00			Jonah sleeping
7:00		4/25	Visit T+K
8:00			kids in garden
10:00			flowers
11:00		4/26	BATH!
14:00			uncle Jeff arrives
15:30			Surf Trip to lighthouse
17:00			drummers @ beach
18:10			waves
20:00			Jeff surfs
25:00		5/10	Plant Garden
29:00		5/14	Plaster hands/feet for Grandma

VIDEOTAPE LOGSHEET   TAPE # _____

start time	end time	date	scene description

© 2008 Rubin   ldvb.blogspot.com   www.nonlinear.info/logsheet.pdf

FIGURE 4.3 I use a videotape logsheet format with columns for start time, end time (which I don't use very much), date, and descriptions. Blank tape log sheets are available in PDF form for downloading at http://ldvb.blogspot.com.

Here is an example of a tape log (see **Figure 4.3**). You don't need to get fancy, but you will have to watch your tape and make some organized notes on this sheet. Keep all your tape logs in a book or at least in a folder. Better yet, here's an assignment for you.

Assignment 9: Making a Log Book

Right now, get any old three-ring binder, no more than 1 inch thick. You can either design the cover and log sheets yourself or use the ones that are on my Web site at www.nonlinear.info/logsheet.pdf and www.nonlinear.info/logcover1.pdf. Place the cover sheet under the plastic on the front of your notebook.

Now print out about 20 copies of the log sheets and place them in your notebook. Use tab dividers to separate the blank log sheets into two or three sections: one marked *M* for "master," one marked *S* for "source," and (if you need it) one marked *A* for "analog." Now you have a handy log book to keep track of your first tapes.

Your logging station

You don't need any fancy setup to log your tapes. In fact, in Chapter 5 I advise doing it away from your editing system, mostly to break up the process physically. (I think it's healthy to cut back on your time in front of a computer.) Logging does not require a computer or even a TV set, although you could use both or either if you so choose. **Figure 4.4** shows my logging station.

FIGURE 4.4 This is my friend Laura pretending to log one of my tapes, while actually demonstrating excellent logging setup and position. You can do it anywhere, and all the materials you need (videotape, log book, pen) are close at hand.

1. Sit down somewhere comfortable with your camera and log book. Place the log book in your lap and open it to a blank page.

2. Flip out the camera's LCD, and turn on the timecode and data code displays (for date).

3. With a nice pen, write the reel number at the top right corner of your new log sheet (so that you can see it easily while flipping pages). Try to write legibly.

4. Rewind the tape to the beginning, and press Play.

5. You should be able to log the tape in real time, as it plays, without making any stops. (You can stop if you want to; you just shouldn't *need* to.)

6. Keep your notes short but descriptive. Focus on *scene changes*— actual events of shooting and the dates shot—not on the detail of the content from each shot or setup.

That's all there is to it.

The time to make a log is the first time you sit down to watch a tape. You can probably tell why you need continuous and ascending timecode; how useful is a log if every series of shots begins again at 00:00?

How much detail to log?

I try to be pretty casual with my logs. The more accurate you try to be, the slower the process and the more likely you are to bag the whole exercise. For S tapes, the most important distinction is to note the scene changes. Don't get too caught up in precisely noting the timecode; it is only there to help you find material on the tape. For instance, ignore the timecode unit of frames. Also, you need to be only reasonably close with the seconds, but do get the minutes right. With a little practice, you can do this while the timecode is displayed, without ever stopping the tape after you press Play. There is nothing wrong with starting and stopping the tape to be more accurate in your logs, but it will slow down the process and establishes a degree of accuracy that is unnecessary. And so, after a little practice, your list might read as follows:

00:00-	11/24/08	Thanksgiving with family
12:30-	11/25/08	Jonah learns to ski
15:40-	12/01/08	Airport coming home
16:30-	12/12/08	Jonah makes a kite

Notice that I didn't use any end times (I only use end times on the clips recorded onto master tapes), and I've kept my descriptions very general. A more accurate but laborious log describing the shots in more detail may or may not help make material easier to edit. For instance:

00:00-	11/24/08	Thanksgiving cooking
02:15-		Dog eats beets sequence
04:10-		Grandpa arrives
09:35-		Cutting the turkey
12:30-	11/25/08	Drive to Ski Mountain
14:10-		WS Summit, Jonah turns
15:40-	12/1/08	Airport, coming home

Storage and Care of Videotapes

Digital videotapes are small and cute, and they don't take up a lot of room even when you have a pile of them sitting on your desk. Until you have collected many of them, a dedicated tape storage container is probably overkill (see **Figure 4.5**). If you purchase tapes in boxes of five, the best solution is to store your tapes in the empty cardboard box as you record them. I rip the top off the box and slide the tapes in.

FIGURE 4.5 Although plenty of companies make fancy tape storage containers—and I've purchased my fair share—this down-home method still works well for me.

You can also see why it's important to have a label on both the top and the side of each tape.

Tape care

What kills tapes?

▶ Sun

▶ Heat

▶ Moisture and humidity

▶ Dust, dirt, and gunk

▶ Magnetic fields

▶ Time

If you want to keep your tapes pristine for a decade or more, consider storing them in airtight containers away from the elements. Professional videotape facilities maintain "tape vaults" (not like a bank vault;

more like a big closet) with temperature and humidity controls. But this is perhaps a bit extreme for our purposes.

Most important, make sure you keep your tapes in their plastic cases whenever they are not in your camera. These cases protect the tapes from direct trauma (like getting stepped on) as well as from most dust and dirt.

Ironically, you must not store your tapes near your desktop computer, television set, or any other equipment that has a CRT screen or audio speakers, because the magnetic fields they produce may cause data loss on the tapes.

Videotape rolls up neatly inside the tiny cassette when the tape's tension is smooth and even. If the tension is off for any reason, there can be bits of slack here and there—especially when you shuttle forward, pause, reverse, play again, reverse again, and so on. All of this direction changing can lead to creases in the tape, and possibly to its permanent and inescapable ruin. Some professionals suggest that when you're done using a tape, you should fast-forward to the end (without watching it) and then rewind it all the way to the beginning, to keep the tension even. I've heard others recommend that you do this once a year to prevent any stickiness from developing.

Rumor has it that, if possible, you should store tapes on end, on their short sides, not flat. That way, if there is any tiny mess-up in rolling the tape on the spool, the weight of the tape will not cause a crease. Yeah, I know it's pretty unlikely. Still, people ask, and I'm here to answer.

When it comes to tape care, I do only three things:

▶ I clean the heads on my camera once every few months.

▶ I religiously keep my tapes in their plastic cases.

▶ I rarely step on them.

NOTE: Sometimes what looks like a bad videotape—with a dropout of sound/image/timecode—is really just a problem with your camcorder. Before you freak out when a tape seems to have gone bad, take a breath, and try the tape in a different player. If the problem follows the tape, you've got a problem.

Other than these things, I'm pretty cavalier about my tape care. I suppose it will take only one ruined tape to get me to do any more than this. A major tape disaster has never happened to me or anyone I know, although I do find the occasional timecode dropout on some of my oldest MiniDV tapes (after nine years), but no video loss or debilitating issues. Yet. But it does happen, so be aware and treat your tapes just as you would your photos or any other irreplaceable personal belongings.

Head-cleaning tapes

Every so often, you'll put in a tape and press Play, but rather than a normal video picture, you see odd blocks or thick bands crisscrossing the screen or bouncing here and there. They look digital, but they are caused by unclean tape heads. Luckily, cleaning the heads is no problem (see **Figure 4.6**).

FIGURE 4.6 A typical head-cleaning tape "rubs" the internal parts of your camera when you press Play. The rubbing process takes only a few seconds, so don't just insert the tape, press play, and walk away. Instead, press Play, count to five, then Stop. If you clean your camera's tape heads once every few months, it should take you a decade to use the thing up. When the tape is at an end, don't rewind it, just toss it.

Disable record (aka "locking" a tape)

After you're finished recording on a tape, take a moment to protect your video.

There's a little switch on the top of DV cassettes that, when flipped, "locks" the tape, making it impossible to record over existing material (see **Figure 4.7**). With this great feature and a little discipline, you can save yourself years of bitter self-recrimination. Whenever I shoot a tape and take it out of the camera, I make sure to lock it. I never used to do this until one memorable day when I accidentally recorded over a few seconds of one of my best videos; I had been showing the tape to some friends earlier and forgot that I had left it in the camera.

I wholeheartedly recommend locking your recorded tapes. If you do, the worst that can happen is that you may try to record, and the tape will tell you it's locked—which means you'll have to eject it, flip the lock switch, and reinsert it in the camera. All my tapes that are in storage and not slated for future use are locked. I say it's worth it.

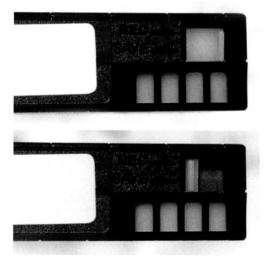

FIGURE 4.7 The tape-protection lock switch on the top of a cassette is accessible once the tape is ejected, even without removing it from the camera. Get in the habit of locking your tapes as soon as you've finished shooting.

Getting Ready to Edit

Shooting is easy. Everyone knows how to use a camera. And if you watch your video only once after you shoot it, there are few consequences for fairly bad shooting. How wonderful!

Editing, on the other hand, is the problem. Most people don't have an intuitive sense of how to edit a video and, therefore, find the idea daunting. You might think that shooting video is for amateurs, but editing it is only for professionals. This isn't true, but I can sympathize with the reasoning. Until very recently, the tools for editing were too complicated for home video enthusiasts to deal with. But organizing and editing your video can be the most satisfying part of the process. Editing tools now on the market—with (I promise) lots more inexpensive products to come—virtually guarantee that editing will be easy for you. But before we start, there are a few little things you need in order to prepare yourself.

The Camera and the Computer

Editing is possible because a camera can connect to a computer in a standard way (remember FireWire?). Let's set up a place where you can edit and watch your videos. It should be almost like your TV setup: You'll want to be comfortable and have lots of high-quality sound and images at your disposal. But it will also be like your office: You'll need a comfortable chair, a modern computer, and some workspace. In the trade-off between comfort and efficiency, I know that efficiency—along with its evil twin, economy—tends to win out. Most of us will edit wherever our computer is sitting. This is OK. You can set up something fancier after you've been editing for a while and are pretty sure that it's your new favorite hobby.

Now, I know that you have a high-powered computer. But I want to talk about your hard disk and storage.

Digital Video Is Big

Write this down—no, better yet, memorize it:

4.5 minutes per gigabyte

The DV format compresses a traditional broadcast-quality video signal to one-fifth the size without sacrificing much in the way of image quality. (The sound remains perfect, by the way, at CD quality.) Once again: *Four and a half minutes of regular DV requires 1 gigabyte of hard disk space.* Say this with confidence at parties, and you'll gain the respect of your geeky friends. I will quiz you on this later.

If you want to really show off your sophistication, you'll also know that you get about

7.0 minutes per gigabyte

of compressed high-definition video on a hard disk. This might strike you as odd—that you get *more* HD than regular old video on a tape—but the HD is compressed more than the regular. Anyway, if you're working in high-def, this 7 minutes per GB number is important.

And regardless of what format you shoot, a few minutes of video per GB is enormous when compared with other files you might have more familiarity with—such as audio (where you might get hours per GB), photos (at a few MB per image, say, you'd hold almost a thousand photos on a GB), or text files (heck, the text contained in this entire book isn't a GB). In the panorama of digital files, video is the big daddy.

Shooting Ratios

When you get down to it, no matter how careful you were during the shoot, you probably recorded plenty of material that shouldn't end up in your finished project. I'll try not to get all mathematical on you, but the ratio of material in your final product to the total amount of footage you shot is called your *shooting ratio*. For instance, if you shot 100 hours of material and were trying to make a 5-minute music video, you would likely go insane because your shooting ratio would be an absurd 1,200:1. More realistically, you might have shot 60 minutes of material (a full DV tape) for that same 5-minute video—a shooting ratio of 12:1. That's still higher than I recommend, but at least now you would be in the ballpark of "normal" ratios.

I think that a shooting ratio between 6:1 and 3:1 is about right for home video. But this number will vary. At any rate, the shooting ratio is not all that important; it's just a good way to begin thinking about a relationship between the footage you've shot and the material in your finished videos.

NOTE: Big-budget Hollywood filmmakers might shoot 50 or even 100 hours of film to get the coverage for a 2-hour-plus final cut—a shooting ratio of between 25:1 and 50:1. Nine to 12 hours of material is required for many 1-hour evening TV shows, with a typical ratio of 10:1. Television commercials are generally the most expensive productions per second; often, several hours of film must be shot for just 30 seconds (900 frames!) of a commercial—a ratio that's off the charts. Documentary filmmakers have radical shooting ratios, too—often shooting many hundreds of hours for their projects. Don't do this. This isn't your career.

Culling vs. editing

Editing serves a number of practical purposes, all of which are valid and important. On every tape you shoot, a lot of the video is either not that good—too much camera movement, poorly lit shots, and the like—or way too repetitive (45 minutes of surfers wiping out). If you do nothing else with editing, at least you should know how to get rid of the unwatchable parts of the tape.

TIP: iMovie and other basic "editing" packages are ideal for culling. They make it easy to get your clips in, winnow out the bad stuff, and save the good parts.

I call this *culling*, meaning you are "throwing out" selected parts of a tape—maybe many of them—to make for easier viewing. It is not really editing, even if you do it with editing software.

I like to think of culling as the "personal" edit. When you have thrown out the bad stuff, what is left is watchable but will probably be interesting only to the people who are in it—or maybe only to you. I could watch hours of my kid, or of my friends hanging out playing guitars, but I wouldn't subject anyone else to such torture. So it's probably not a good idea to distribute videos cut only to this degree. Even if you don't want to do full-blown editing, you can cull your material to a more manageable amount—say, 60 minutes of original footage down to 20 minutes—without a lot of effort.

Editing, then, is what you do with the culled footage. If you know you'll be editing a video, however, you don't need to do a separate culling pass; it can all be done at once. It is through editing that your video becomes ready for public scrutiny. This is the process that takes whatever material you've shot and knocks it down to between 2 and 5 minutes long. You cannot do this simply by getting rid of bad material—**you'll also need to cut out *good* material to make the remaining video *better*.** Many beginners find it difficult to throw out "good" video. I guess the best response I have is this: You're not *really* throwing anything out (it's all shot on digital tape, and the material on the original tape is never touched).

Assuming you have appropriate coverage, the less material you shoot for a project, the easier it will be to edit. Conversely, knowing what you need to construct a good-looking finished video makes shooting easier; as you get better at editing, you will get better at shooting too. This is why many Hollywood editors often end up as very good directors.

Cabling

So much of the comfort that comes with understanding video, and computers in general, is rooted in a familiarity with the various cables they use. If you will take a moment to learn just a bit about cables and their connectors, you may be amazed to find that a world of complex things you used to avoid has suddenly become logical and simple. Knowing your cables will make you a whiz in your friends' eyes, more fun at parties, and probably loads more comfortable next time you hook up a DVR, DVD player, or stereo system.

Cables and terminals

Cables are composed of strands of metal wiring and protective shielding and insulation, usually wrapped up in a neat rubber-hose package. Wires come in a variety of gauges (thicknesses) and materials, all of which affect how much electricity or data they can carry without overheating. Shielding is a critical component of cabling: It prevents the electromagnetic fields generated by the cables from interfering with things (house wiring, recording devices, the delicate tissues of your brain...) on the outside. Cheap cables often have only minimal gauge and marginal shielding; two seemingly identical cables can have significantly different prices, simply due to variations in the quality of the materials used.

The metal doohickies on the end of any cable are known as *terminals* or *connectors*. To have a basic understanding of the subject, you must first learn the difference between *male* and *female* connectors: Male connectors tend to poke outward, and female connectors are those with one or more receptacles awaiting something to be inserted. (If this concept still perplexes you, go ask your parents.)

Here is my list of the top six most important cables for the home-video enthusiast, along with their associated connector variations:

▶ Plain ol' audio/video

▶ Coaxial

▶ FireWire

▶ S-Video

▶ USB-2

▶ Power (AC or DC-with-adapter)

Plain ol' audio/video: These cables usually come in a bundle of either two or three strands. Two-strand cables can be used for stereo sound (left and right audio) or for video and a monaural audio track. Far more useful is the three-strand variety: Output from editing systems, and subsequent input to VCRs, DVRs, tuners, or TV sets, tends to run in three tracks (video and left and right stereo audio) and so need the three lines.

Audio/video cables are relatively inexpensive and generally come with any camera, TV set, game console, or stereo system you buy. I've thrown away more audio/video cables than I've ever used. Now I keep a little box of them in various lengths, because it's so nice to have these handy when I need one.

Audio/video cables have the greatest variety of potential connectors on the ends. The most common is the *RCA connector*.

While RCA connectors are common for audio (more specifically, *unbalanced* audio, for the sophisticated among you), they can also be used for video. A variation on the RCA plug is the *RCA mini-jack* (also called the *headphone jack* or *1/4-inch jack*), which is enormously popular these days for analog output on all sorts of consumer devices.

TIP: If you look closely at the male end of the RCA mini-jack, you'll notice that for each connector on the other end of the cable there is a little groove in the silver plug—and thus the three-stranded (video+stereo audio) cable has three grooves. But a simple headphone plug would have two, for left and right audio.

Coaxial ("coax"): Coaxial is a remarkably versatile cable, moving video and audio signals in a highly shielded set of wires. Coax cables tend to cost more than the less-shielded alternatives, but they are the standard for professionals and are common in homes wired for cable television. They are made of a thin-gauge center wire surrounded by insulation and a braid of shielding metal. Inexpensive coax may use aluminum braids; higher-priced versions provide better shielding with copper braids. Coax delivers cable TV to millions of homes throughout the United States.

NOTE: Cables may have different connectors on either end, effectively translating from, say, three RCA plugs (video, left and right audio) into a single RCA mini. Thus, a cable can act as a sort of extension cord (when it's the same on both ends)—or, in other configurations, a translation cord.

You may recognize the familiar coax connector on the back of your old TV set or cable box: It has a little hole for the wire, in the middle of a larger

boltlike stump. Cables slide over the bolt, and either are held on only by friction or have a threaded connector that screws onto the connector like a jar lid.

FireWire (IEEE 1394, iLink): A FireWire cable is a small bundle of wires (in a single sheath) that carry digital data at a bandwidth of 400 to 800 Mbps—plenty fast for digital video (which transfers at 25 Mbps). FireWire connects digital cameras to computers, but it can also be used anywhere that a high-bandwidth connection is needed, such as between mass-storage devices and computers.

There are two main varieties of FireWire connectors: 4-pin and 6-pin. The 4-pin type is common in cameras and other DV devices. The 6-pin type, which is shaped like a little *D*, is indigenous to Apple hardware.

4-pin FireWire   *6-pin FireWire*

S-Video: A kind of analog video cable, S-Video provides higher-quality video signals than the simpler "plain ol'" video cable described above. I almost didn't include S-Video in this list as I don't use it very often, mostly because it requires a type of cable I don't usually have sitting around. If you use S-Video at all, it may be for taking the analog video signal out of your digital camcorder (assuming it has an S-Video plug) and connecting it to an analog S-Video-compatible recording device, such as an old S-VHS or Hi-8 camcorder). Because S-Video cables handle only video, they still must be used in conjunction with some other type of cabling to manage the audio portion of the program.

Composite vs. Component Video

There are primarily two flavors of video in entertainment systems and cameras. One is called *composite* video. It mixes up all the signals that make up a video and runs them through a single cable. Composite video is convenient and inexpensive, but it's of relatively low quality. On the other end of the range is *component* video. It separates the three "components" of video (don't ask what they are— the explanation is really technical) and runs them in three pathways within and between video devices. Component video is inconvenient and expensive, but it provides exceptional quality.

A hybrid of component and composite is commonly called *S-Video*. It splits the video signal into two parts—better than only one (composite), but not as good as three (component). S-Video allows a significant improvement in quality with a modest adjustment in price.

S-Video connectors are standardized and are visible on many DV cameras. Here is mine:

USB: For a long time, computers sported a USB plug for devices that didn't need to move much data around very quickly, and the maximum rate of flow was less than 12 Mbps. This was fine for connecting a keyboard or mouse. But more recently, USB was improved (sometimes called "high-speed USB" or "USB 2.0"), providing for data rates of 480 Mbps. The connector and cable look the same, but more data can move through these quickly. Since they approach FireWire in this capability, you won't often see a peripheral device with both FireWire

and USB connectors. And while USB might be used to move data from a camcorder into a computer, it would be less likely to be used to play video from a camera to a computer (which requires not just data transfer, but smooth continuous data transfer). Nonetheless, it is increasingly popular on consumer devices.

When USB is used on peripheral devices (camcorders in particular), it often appears in a smaller form:

Power: You already know all you need to about power cords. I mention them here only because it's very nice when a camera can charge up its batteries while they are attached to the camera. This way, you can have the camera plugged in while you edit, and at the same time be prepping the camera for your next video shoot.

The most useful cable

I think the most useful cable for DV is this one:

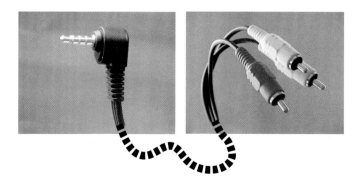

It takes analog video out of your camera and readies it to go into any number of standard, common devices—for me, a television, or a tuner of some kind that might lead to your TV and speakers. No matter how digital things get, as long as there is still analog equipment you might want to connect to, you'll want to keep this cable handy. It's such an important cable for consumers, I think it should have an official name: How about *analog DV cable*? That works.

Hooking everything up

For your entire video system to work, just one thing needs to happen: You must connect the camera to the computer with a FireWire cable. The only two possible additions to this step are (1) plugging your camera into its power source so that it doesn't run out of juice while you're working, and (2) piping the analog video signal out of your camera (if you want) and plugging it into a television monitor.

The secret to hooking everything up properly is knowing (1) what is *video*, what is *audio*, and what is *both*; (2) which plugs are IN and which are OUT; and (3) how to recognize what kinds of cable and connector are required. With this knowledge under your belt, you'll have no problems with hookup. Of course, many products fail to give much direction of this sort; they may provide an Audio/Video label next to a little hole, but they don't specify what *kind* of audio/video plug it is, or whether the stream is flowing in or out. And if you don't recognize a little hole as needing a male RCA mini-jack, asking for what you need at your local electronics store can turn into a ridiculous comedy: "Hi, I'm looking for a long cable that has a little thing on the end with a ring around it...and, uh, three bigger red, white, and...I think yellow..."

TIP: Rules of thumb: (1) Unless you have a specific notice to the contrary, holes not labeled In or Out are both. (2) There are also usually multiple plugs that do similar things, just in different formats. Thus, an S-Video plug provides analog in/out, as does the little headphone jack near it, labeled Audio/Video. Both are analog, and both are in/out. The only difference is the format.

My old camcorder all wired up: power, FireWire to the computer, analog video to a monitor, headphones for me.

Surprise Quiz

I told you there'd be a quiz. You should be able to do this in your head.

How many minutes of standard video can you store on an 80 GB hard disk?

How many minutes of HD video can you store on a 100 GB hard disk?

Extra Credit: How much hard disk space is required to hold 15 minutes of regular video?

Your "Edit Bay"

Because professionals spend all day editing, and the equipment can be expensive, they often rent editing rooms specifically designed for both efficiency and comfort. These rooms, called *edit bays*, are dark and cool and cozy and are often equipped with a dedicated countertop, a bunch of monitors, a special keyboard, nice speakers, and a comfy sofa in the back so the director/producer/client can recline, sip sodas, chat on the phone, and watch what's going on, all at the same time. You don't need to build a whole "bay," but if video is your hobby, you'll want to have an appropriate workspace for editing.

Monitors

As long as you have a camera, all it takes to set up your editing system is a single computer with a single computer monitor. I edit all the time on my laptop—by the pool, in the car, on the plane. This setup works fine, but in some cases it's more complicated than that.

On the left, a professional video editing bay in Hollywood. On the right, a makeshift editing bay for an independent feature film, circa 2003: The hardware changes color and horsepower, but the setup is essentially the same.

An analog video monitor is not the same thing as a digital computer monitor. Even though they can look very similar, there are important differences between the two, most of which are highly technical. Among the differences: Computer screens show an image all at once (called *progressive scanning*), whereas analog TV screens present an image drawn rapidly by interwoven scan lines (*interlaced scanning*); computer monitors have square pixels, but video monitors have rectangular pixels; and computer screens have resolutions that can vary (for example, 1280 by 1024, 1024 by 768, or 1600 by 1200), whereas television monitors effectively have a fixed resolution of 640 by 480. And this doesn't even touch on the issues of color space!

Suffice it to say, it is extraordinarily challenging to play a video that looks "right" on both a TV set and a computer screen. But all this is changing right now. With the advent of digital television broadcasts

NOTE: This, by the way, is what the *I* and *P* stand for in descriptions of HiDef video. On the one hand, you'll see *1080i*, which means there are 1,080 lines of video (which is good), but they are interlaced (which many consider inferior). On the other hand you might also see *720p*, which means there are fewer lines of video than on the 1080 display, but the display shows them progressively, which looks nicer and, some say, more filmlike. The ideal would be 1080p, a format that would trump both of these. That's what a Blu-ray DVD is playing, and with luck, your display can present this quality.

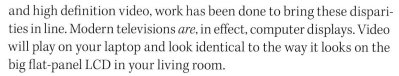

TIP: If you still watch your videos on a traditional analog TV, you should probably loop your video through your camera to a regular TV while you're editing.

and high definition video, work has been done to bring these disparities in line. Modern televisions *are*, in effect, computer displays. Video will play on your laptop and look identical to the way it looks on the big flat-panel LCD in your living room.

As a rule of thumb, you want to be able to see the video you are editing in a format that most closely resembles what will be seen when it is finally distributed—that is, on a typical display. If you edit with tiny images, you'll miss elements and timings that you would have seen on a normal-sized display. Consequently, to the degree possible, you want to be able to review your editing work full screen. And in a perfect world, you'd be watching it full screen most of the time.

So, at least when you're starting out, one computer monitor can adequately serve dual purposes. But if it is possible, it's best to have two displays, one for editing and one for viewing. It also lets you spread out your workspace.

Looping analog video

From a wiring standpoint, using a video monitor complicates matters, although the logic is pretty straightforward. The computer and its monitor are a kind of closed system; there is often no direct way to get a video image out of a computer and insert it into a TV. But remember, you will use the FireWire cable to connect a camera to this computer. The addition of your camera is what expands your options. The camera not only provides a DV input but also allows DV output, so you can record rough cuts or finished cuts back onto your DV tape to your heart's content. But it serves another purpose as well, and this is the important part: The camera works as a digital-to-analog converter. Many cameras have two kinds of analog video in/out plugs—S-Video and RCA mini.

By taking the video/audio output through the RCA mini plug, you now have a fairly good-quality analog signal that can be pumped directly into a TV set or entertainment system/tuner—or, in case you want to record an analog dub, input into a VHS-format VCR or camcorder.

Chairs

I think it's important to have enough room for two in any space where editing takes place. You don't need a sofa behind you, but a second chair comes in handy when you want to show a video to friends and family before you've dubbed it to tape and taken it to the TV room.

For a while, my editing bay was set up *in* my family TV room. The home television set also served (quite efficiently) as my video monitor. But the room simply wasn't comfortable enough for editing. It was a great place, however, for kicking back and watching the videos, so editing in there was *almost* worth the ergonomic challenges.

Camcorders are so portable that you can edit wherever your computer happens to be, record the cut to DV tape, take the camera (along with the appropriate video cable) over to your TV set, and set up the screening in a comfortable viewing space.

Dubbing Old Analog Tapes

Going digital can be a big decision. If this isn't your first camcorder, you probably have a pile of analog videotapes sitting around—never edited, and probably unwatched for ages.

You don't need to use an outside service for this task. Converting analog tapes to digital is eminently doable. It involves watching the tapes—a good idea anyway, so that you can log them as they're dubbed.

How to Dub

Almost every DV camera comes with a receptacle for an analog input/output cable. You can use it for output to a VCR to make a VHS tape or to a television set for viewing. But when you use it for input to the camera, it will perform analog-to-digital conversion.

1. Hook up the output connector of your VCR (or analog camcorder) to the analog port in your DV camera, using our aforementioned "analog DV cable."

2. Set the DV camera to VCR mode.

3. Turn on the timecode display. This is a good idea in this situation, because you'll be logging the dub while it is being recorded.

4. Get your blank log sheet ready.

5. Put a clean DV tape in your camera. Label it something like *A1*, and label your log sheet with the same name.

6. Press Record on the DV camera. Wait until the timecode reads 3 seconds or so; then press Pause. Now you're ready to start playing the analog tape.

7. Make sure the tape you want to dub is in the VCR or analog camcorder and that it is rewound to the beginning. Then press Play on the analog device. In a couple of seconds the tape will start playing.

8. Depending on your mood, either release the Pause button on the DV camera as soon as you press Play on the analog tape side, or wait until you see the first image pop up on the camera's LCD. I like to get every frame, so I do the former.

9. Now the dub is in progress. You should see the red light on the DV camera's LCD, indicating that it's recording, and the images from the analog tape should be displaying there, too. Start making notes on your log sheet—what you see, the timecodes, that sort of thing.

Make sure the DV camera is not connected to your computer during the analog-to-digital conversion process. When the FireWire cable is connected, it's possible that the analog signal will not be recognized and the camera will appear to have no video coming into it. Disconnecting the FireWire cable will force the camera to look elsewhere for video, which it will find coming from the analog cable input.

Choosing What to Edit

As I said before, not everything you shoot will be edited. When you are shooting, you usually won't know when you have enough good coverage to give you something editable. When I review and log my material, I look for a few hallmarks that will drive me to edit one project over another:

▶ **Is the content compelling?** It doesn't have to be footage of a train wreck or an alien landing to be compelling to my family, but it should have some intrinsic merit—something that entices me to cut it together and that others may want to see. (If I'm interested enough to spend a few hours editing a video, I can usually find a willing audience to view it.)

▶ **Do I have the structure?** I want to know that some of my material lends itself to being a beginning, middle, and end. I can fudge a little here; it is not uncommon simply to fade up and call some random shot "the beginning." But it's best if the material supports a little natural structure and if there is actually something driving the video forward—say, a joke or a moment that could serve as the climax or punch line.

▶ **Do I have the coverage?** It doesn't take much—a simple shot/reverse shot, maybe a good master shot with a few nice inserts—to give you the kind of material you need to make smooth edits.

▶ **Is the photography attractive?** Once you shoot a fair amount of video, you'll begin to be discerning about the quality of the video you shoot. Some interesting videos are ruined (or at least impeded) by lousy lighting and framing. Personally, I am drawn to spend my time editing videos that not only have interesting content but also happen to look nice. It's not a deal breaker, but it's one factor I consider when deciding what to edit.

▶ **Does it fit within my limits?** Do I have 10 to 20 minutes of footage that could nicely go together as a single project? Sometimes I will shoot something, maybe 5 minutes of bits, and not really have enough to merit an edit session. Then something else happens later—another scene, really, but one that sort of goes with the other, and it's perhaps 15 minutes long—and I realize that I could put these two short bits together and make an even better video. As long as the sum total of raw material you intend to capture is less than 20 minutes, you can get away with a lot of odd bits strung together to make a neat final video. For instance, I shot about 10 minutes of footage for my birthday party last year—only enough for a tiny finished video. But I noticed that, on the same tape a day earlier, I had shot another 10 minutes as I moved around the house, cleaning and preparing and playing with my son. Although these bits were quite different from my birthday footage, they all went together well for a little video project.

The raw material does not need to satisfy all of the above criteria. I often decide to edit something based purely on my desire to play around with it, and without regard for whether or not I have the proper structure or coverage. But it's best to think of all these criteria to ensure a successful project. If not, you may find yourself with 20 minutes of digital video in your computer and no idea how to make it better.

Capturing Video

The process of getting digital video into a computer for editing is called *capturing the video*. It can be as simple as playing a videotape in your camera and clicking a button on your computer screen that tells it, in effect, "Grab this."

Back when video was only analog, getting it into a computer meant *digitizing* it. The process generally requires all kinds of tricky hardware and confusing software settings to get right, and it is something best left up to computer geeks.

DV eliminates the need to digitize. The FireWire cable makes connecting a digital camera to a computer almost effortless. Thus, capturing digital video is reasonably intuitive. Although technically it is like

TIP: Clearly, if you're using a tapeless camcorder, there is no special issue with "capturing" video—you plug your camera into your computer and transfer the digital files from one device to the other. They move intact, just like any other digital file. You can also selectively move them to your computer, and not grab them all if you want. But if you don't move them, you'll probably lose them.

doing any large file transfer (say, from CD to hard drive), the process of moving DV into a computer is more like playing a videotape than transferring a file.

There are two ways to capture digital video—the *fast fun way*, and the *slow ridiculous way*. (These are not the technical terms, in truth; I just made them up.) The slow ridiculous way (or *SRW*) is also known as *batch capturing* or *capturing with timecode*. The gist of SRW is that you play through your tape, selecting places on it (identified by way of timecode) containing shots you want to get into the computer. You can select shots one at a time, then have the computer take control and capture each one; or you can shuttle through your entire tape, marking beginning and end frames to indicate the shots you like, and when you are finished, you can have the computer automatically rewind the tape and begin a long process of getting everything captured for you.

The SRW method is, of course, slow (you start and stop the tape over and over). In addition, it might require two passes through the tape— once for you to find shots, and once more for the computer to get the shots—and involves a fair amount of camera-to-computer work. And it only works if you have perfect timecode.

The fast fun way (or *FFW*) is also called *capturing on the fly*. I like the sound of that. "On the fly" means you simply click a button when you want to start capturing, and click another button when you want to stop (see **Figure 5.1**). Man, is that simple. The timecode is there and is important, but you don't need it in your face, even for capturing. In one pass, and usually with minimal starting and stopping of the tape, you've not only screened your video but also got it in the computer. The FFW method takes probably about one-third the time of the SRW, and is better for the long-term health of both tape and camera.

FIGURE 5.1 Final Cut Express's capturing window is sophisticated: It lets you control many aspects of the capture, such as how the computer labels a clip and where the clip goes, and it offers a series of fine controls for selecting the beginning and ending frames. I suggest ignoring most of these features, except the Reel number (you'll see it here filled in on the right: *S08.04*). At the bottom right is a series of capturing options; I like "Now."

Learn how your particular editing software captures on the fly. This is the basis for getting video into the computer. But know this: Any time a computer sees that you want to capture video, it should want to know a bunch of things about what you are capturing. It will want to know the reel number of the tape; it will ask about scene, take, and other odd data; it will allow you to type in descriptions; and so on. You can ignore all of the software's requests and features but one: the reel number. The computer needs to know what reel it's working on. With a reel number and a timecode reference (which the computer can read itself and is always watching), all the information you need is right there in the computer. You have a log sheet full of shot descriptions, and because you are doing small projects you simply don't need to waste time typing in a lot of details. Get the video in quickly, easily, and with minimal typing or computer-in-your-face stuff.

In Hollywood, video is captured take by take. Every take is its own little video file. And even most beginners will work this way, because it feels natural and logical to simply grab the bits you think you want and use them in your edit. But *you* are about to do something radical and completely different: You're going to capture all your video in one giant chunk.

OK, remember how you previously shot 10 to 20 minutes of material? Some of it is good and some of it is bad, and regardless of whether you intend to just cull it or give it a real edit, you'll want the entire thing in the computer before working with it.

This method is based on a few details worth mentioning:

▶ It wouldn't be reasonable to capture *all* your material if hard disk space weren't so cheap. Just a few years ago a gigabyte of storage cost much more than it does today, so you would try to capture only the video you wanted to use; all that garbage video was wasting valuable space. But today it's difficult to find a hard disk that's under 80 GB—and that's enough space for many hours of DV. You now have room for the whole thing. And more.

▶ Shuttling a camera around, looking for shots that are good and ignoring those that are bad, and capturing only the good ones— that *is* editing. Get it in the computer first; *then* separate out the good and the bad.

▶ Lots of shuttling forward and backward and stopping and starting isn't healthy for either your tapes or your camera. Why put them through so much when you really don't have to?

Let's get started capturing your video. Find the beginning of the material you want to work with, start playing it back on your camera, click the Capture button on your computer screen, and let that sucker roll until you get to the end.

Tips

▶ If the **end** means the video is going to roll into a non-timecode part of the tape, this **could** be a problem, depending on your software. Always start and stop on a frame with timecode. This may mean that you must either stop capturing before the end of your material, or make sure you have something—anything— recorded after your material on the tape, so that when you see it you can stop capturing.

▶ If you really, really know that a lot of your video is garbage and there is simply no point in capturing it, then by all means feel free to stop capturing when the garbage starts coming in, and start again when it has passed. This approach has several advantages: It consumes less hard disk space, results in smaller files, and makes it a little easier to find a shot or scene you're looking for. But even though those benefits sound good, work this way only if it really is easier for you.

I have found no faster or more efficient way to get from shooting to editing than streamlining the capture process. By eliminating typed logs in the computer, by capturing on the fly, by capturing in one (or a few) large chunks of video, you get your material into the computer as quickly as possible. For every 20 minutes of raw video, you'll want to spend about 20 minutes getting it ready to edit. Remember, your *continuous timecode* makes all of this possible on any computer and with any editing software. Without good continuous timecode, organizing your video is harder, and coming back to a project years later is practically impossible.

iMovie Caveat

With all the nice things I could say about Apple's iMovie, I must insist that it is actually designed quite poorly when it comes to efficient editing. In an effort to make it easy to use for most people with camcorders (and it *is* easy to use), many standard features of editing software have been obscured or eliminated such that using it for basic editing can be harder if not altogether impossible.

If you want to edit using iMovie, I would recommend using a version before 2008, like iMovie HD (from 2007). That version of iMovie lets you edit pretty well, and it has a number of nice features. Still, I believe iMovie is actually harder to use than Apple's Final Cut Express. For instance, iMovie is great for managing your video clips if you don't edit at all, and it's really great for culling tapes from long boring footage to a shorter batch. But if you're interested in basic *editing*, Final Cut Express can be used in a very simple mode, ignoring many of its advanced features, to make for quick and highly professional-looking editing.

Editing

What can I say? Editing is where it all comes together—all the care you took in shooting, all the organizing, all that cool equipment you bought. Editing may seem like the hard part, but it's really not that difficult, and you probably already know more about it than you think. We live in a video-literate culture, and you may well take to this skill like a duck to water. So get a hold of any editing software that you think suits your needs, and then dig in.

NOTE: It may be hard to imagine, but there was a time before editing. It had to be invented. In the earliest days of filmmaking, people just turned the camera on and let life flow by (not entirely unlike many home videos). And it was gripping stuff—like getting a shave or mixing a drink. Most people imagined that following a film would be impossible if the camera jumped to another vantage point or cheated time by cutting ahead in the action.

In a way, editing was one of the first "special effects." But after a few decades of movies, editing caught on and became the norm. And thus, *not* editing your video is a little like purposely living without a car or electricity: There's nothing wrong with not having it, but the advantages of having it are significant.

Who Needs Editing?

You need editing.

For home video, you need it for two primary purposes: to get rid of the bad stuff in the material you've shot, and to construct a little something with the remainder. Editing is the art and craft of doing these things. It can make the difference between a video that's watchable and one that's not.

If recording a moving image is *capturing* time, then editing is *cheating* time. If you want the power to tell stories, create moods, and make time speed up or slow down, you must learn how to edit. It is a totally different skill than shooting (which is a lot like photography), and it is not like writing. If you've watched TV or movies, you have a good idea of what video looks like when it is edited. That's a good start.

Not Everything Gets Edited, Part 2

In case you missed it before, I want to say it again: You will shoot projects that you never edit. The fact is, you don't know what footage you will capture when you turn on the camera. The content may be boring (like when your one-year-old son was about to take his first step, but ended up standing still for ten minutes), or you simply may not have enough coverage.

In addition, not everything *should* be edited. Wanting to tell a story is just one reason to edit. You might simply cull material down to smaller batches or more watchable moments. This results in a form of raw footage that stores well and is never turned into anything with a "structure." It's not a problem to be solved. Just be OK with it.

Editing Terms and Concepts

This chapter is not intended to replace learning how to use your editing application. You'll need to play around with the software a bit and maybe read the manual. But, just as with cameras, most editing packages have some fundamental features in common—whether they're designed for the absolute beginner or the Academy Award–winning professional. Here are a few key software features and editing concepts that should prove useful.

Sync sound

I hope this doesn't come as a shock to anyone, but picture and sound are two completely different forms of media. When you hear sound come out of people's mouths in the movies, what is really happening is this: The pictures were shot with no sound, and the sound was recorded with no picture, and the two have been synchronized and are playing back together. This is called *sync sound*.

Your DV camera records sound at the same time it records the picture. It records both onto the same tape and then plays them back synchronized. So why give this a thought? Because most of the complexity of editing (even at the hobbyist level) comes from managing the two tracks—pictures and sound—and keeping them in sync with each other. If you keep them together, working with pictures and sound is easy, but you miss much of the power of editing.

Consequently, you will sometimes want to separate picture from sound while editing and manage them independently. Let's say you have a shot of me talking, and in the middle of it you want to see my hands (you like the sound, but want to change a bit of picture). Or you may have shot a beautiful mountain vista as a plane was flying overhead, polluting your sound (you like the picture but want to remove the plane noise). Both these examples involve changing one track but not the other, and keeping everything in sync after the change.

At any rate, I just wanted to introduce you to the idea of sync sound, because it will come up later in your editing experiences.

Rippling/not rippling

Think of the shots you are cutting together as a stack of kid's blocks. You put the first one down on the ground, then add the next one on top of the first, and so on. If you pull out a block from the middle of the stack (carefully), all the blocks above it will drop down to fill the space.

A set of video clips stacked up. Pull one out, and they can either stay in place (not ripple) or slide down to fill the gap (ripple).

If you stick a block into the middle of the stack, it shoves all the blocks above a little higher up.

In editing, this effect of pushing up or dropping down is called *rippling*. It means that adjusting one shot doesn't change the shots after it, but it does change *when* they occur.

In most editing systems, when you delete a shot, all the shots after it will "slide" down so that there is no gap. If you lengthen a shot, all following shots will get shoved out.

This may seem like no big deal, but it allows an editor to decide how to adjust something in a sequence. Most consumer-oriented editing software will ripple all the time. To do slightly more advanced editing, you must be able to control this ability—in particular as you work with picture and sound separately.

Reading a shot

Reading a shot refers to the time it takes for the viewer's eyes to scan an image and the brain to comprehend it. In fact, sometimes an image is flashed so quickly that viewers recognize what they saw only a moment or two after it is gone (an interesting psychological effect). The idea of reading a shot is important when you edit because it'll help you figure out how long to leave a bit of video onscreen.

Wide shots take longer to read than close-ups. The more detail in a shot—the more little things the eye must find and the brain must process—the longer the shot should be onscreen. When movies are shown on large theater screens, it can take a viewer many seconds to read a wide shot. But when viewed on television, even though the bits are smaller and may be harder to see, it takes less time to read those same shots. This is why (theoretically) you would edit something differently for a theater than for television. You should edit for how your friends will see your video—probably on a TV monitor.

Source and master

Source material is the raw video you have captured into your computer. It is, by definition, unedited. It may be one shot or many. There are a number of terms that apply equally well to source material, including *source footage*, *raw footage*, and *dailies*. All describe video that you start with.

Once you are building something out of source material, you are editing it "into" a sequence. This sequence might be casually referred to as a *scene,* it might be called a *cut*, and hard-core geeks might call it an EDL (for "edit decision list"). In editing software, the sequence is also known as the *master*. It is correct to say, for instance, "Cut that source shot into the master after the first wide shot."

The term *master* has a number of different meanings, depending on the context. But it is still technically correct to refer to video—particularly in the windows of an editing program—as either source or master. When the editing software has only one preview window, it will alternately show source or master depending on what you are actively selecting at the time. When there are two windows onscreen, one will always be for watching source material and the other for previewing the cut (see **Figure 6.1**).

Timeline

A fundamental element of an editing program's interface is a graphical representation of the sequence you are cutting. This is called a *timeline*. Starting on the left, the timeline begins at time 00:00; as shots are added to the timeline, you can see their corresponding rectangles stacking up and "building out"—a little like film when you cut and tape shots together. The length of a rectangle in the timeline is proportional to the length of time it takes to watch that shot. Long shots have longer rectangles than short shots. There is always a line that rolls over the timeline to indicate where you are now (what you are seeing on the display); it is called something like the *now line* or *playhead.*

FIGURE 6.1 Apple's Final Cut Express, like other serious editing tools (such as Adobe Premiere or Apple's Final Cut Pro), offers a traditional two-window organizational structure. When there are two windows, source material tends to be on the left and master (cut) material on the right. The timeline usually runs along the bottom.

The timeline gives you a sense of what you are cutting, the order of shots, and how long they are, relative to one another. You can always zoom in or out of the timeline to make the scale larger or smaller, depending on how much you want to see in the window at one time.

For beginners, a timeline can be a rather abstract concept, particularly if you can't visualize a real piece of cut film. Another way to view your sequence is a *storyboard*: large image icons representing the first frame of a shot that let you visualize the edit, shot by shot. A storyboard is a far less abstract way to see your sequence, but it doesn't give you any sense of the duration of these shots (relative to one another or to your entire sequence). It also doesn't allow you the opportunity to visualize where picture cuts happen in relation to items in the sound track—an important consideration as you expand your editing abilities.

Top is a timeline from typical prosumer editing software; below are our kid's blocks. Your individual shots in the timeline are like these blocks. You can change their size, slide them around, remove them, and ripple or not ripple that which follows, depending on your needs. In the timeline, the picture (blue) track is above two sound tracks (green).

Editing functions (inserts and trims)

There are really only two kinds of edits you have to make. The first thing you'll want to do is take a new clip and place it into a sequence somewhere. This is known as *inserting*. You may insert a clip at the end of a sequence, or you might want to insert it somewhere in the middle. You could insert between two clips, or maybe insert at some chosen location within a clip you are watching. Regardless of where a shot is placed into the master, the act is still called *inserting*.

The second kind of edit takes any shot in a sequence and changes the frame that it starts or ends on. This amounts to lengthening or shortening a shot and is called *trimming*. (It's unfortunate that the word *trim* sounds like it is only about shortening; in editing, it's not.) Every editing package must provide some method for trimming shots.

Get comfortable trimming and inserting with your editing software. These functions are the bulk of what editing is all about.

A Word About "Editing Tips"

I was very tempted to create a section here called something like "Power DV Editing" or "Hot Editing Tricks from the Pros." But I didn't. Not that tricks aren't important; keyboard shortcuts and macros can make much of the tedium of editing go away. But I think that such tips miss the point. Editing *is* easy. Even back in the days when it was done with a razor blade and a roll of tape, it may have been slow, but it was still pretty easy to do.

Even though the computer provides so many different tools, you won't be using all that many of them. You only need to know how to cut shots together and trim the connection points between shots. As you become more experienced, you may also want to know how to control pictures and sound separately; good editing software allows you to do this kind of thing easily. But be careful not to focus on the wrong features. For now, any editing program will provide the simple tools that are sufficient for our needs.

Track controls

While it's easy to imagine that picture and sound are a single entity recorded together on a bit of videotape, they are, as you now know, separable and distinct. The picture goes in a picture track and the sound in a sound track. So when you play your video, you are actually playing two tracks that are locked together (for the moment).

These tracks are like stacked layers, with the picture track on top and the sound track beneath (an arrangement that leads to editing expressions like, "Lay that sound down underneath this picture"). As a beginner, you'll want to know how to turn a track on or off (to play a sequence with or without the sound). When you get more advanced, you may want to *lock* a track so that its contents don't change but you still see or hear what's on it. Track controls tend to be associated with the graphical display of the tracks—that is, the timeline (see **Figure 6.2**).

FIGURE 6.2 Very basic editing software will pretend that there's only one primary track, composed of video and audio together. When you make edits, you make them in both together. That's how iMovie works, for instance. With a more sophisticated package like Final Cut Express, it's possible to make edits in only one track at a time. The track controls are at the far left, and have three modes: on, off, and on-but-locked. You can have as many audio or video tracks as you need. Video comes into the computer as video and stereo audio (V1 and A1+A2); titles tend to go above V1, and music and other added sounds end up on A3 and down.

Media files vs. project files

Editing software is still just software. When you open an application and create a new video project, you are creating a workspace where all your raw source clips and edited sequences are orchestrated. That workspace doesn't take up much room on your hard disk; it's the digital video files that are really large. *(Remember, 4.5 minutes of video per gigabyte of storage space.)* So let's now make a distinction. A project contains two distinct kinds of files: media files—the big part—which are the actual video; and the project information—the small part—which is just data about the video (how you've chosen to edit it, where the material came from, which effects you've applied to it, and so on). Editing software stores these two types of files separately; consequently, you can delete the media (video or audio) files to free up hard disk space, while still keeping the project files on the computer. You can't tell that these two kinds of files are separate while you use your editing software—in fact, it's really only clear when you look carefully at the contents of your hard disk.

Name	▲	Date Modified	Size	Kind
1 Audio Track		May 28, 2008, 1:20 PM	32.7 MB	AIFF Audio File
2 Audio Track		May 28, 2008, 1:20 PM	24 MB	AIFF Audio File
cree.fcp		Today, 12:18 AM	220 KB	Final Cut Express Project File
Finished Videos.fcp		Today, 12:18 AM	1.4 MB	Final Cut Express Project File
raw		May 22, 2008, 10:49 AM	5.52 GB	QuickTime Movie
raw2		May 22, 2008, 2:43 PM	2.51 GB	QuickTime Movie
song of cruz		May 22, 2008, 9:37 AM	532.6 MB	QuickTime Movie
tapeS06.05		May 8, 2008, 4:11 PM	2.67 GB	QuickTime Movie
tapeS06.05b		May 8, 2008, 4:30 PM	366.9 MB	QuickTime Movie
ZooDay		Aug 3, 2001, 10:24 PM	80 KB	Final Cut Express Project File

I had to construct this illustration because the raw video files on my Mac were in a separate location on my hard disk from the project files. Very separate. But here they are together for you; notice that the tape files are hundreds of MB or several GB large, whereas the project files are thousands of times smaller.

Output (to tape)

Once you've finished editing a sequence, there must always be a way to output the video in real time to an awaiting digital camcorder. This is not the same as an "export" function; it is more akin to the real-time capturing you did to get video into your computer in the first place, but now it's heading out, not in. Whatever software you use, familiarize yourself with its output options and, in particular, the way you archive your final video to tape. Even if you're planning on burning DVDs or uploading to YouTube, you will be glad you have a master tape.

Rubin's Rules of Editing

Ah, more rules. Maybe *rules* is the wrong word. Would it be better if I called them *meditations*? Don't worry, though—they aren't difficult.

1. Editing is about *source management.*

   This is a fancy way of saying that if you don't know what material you have, you can't edit it. Know your footage—where it is located (using timecode, log sheets, and labeled tapes) and what it looks like. The more familiar you are with the material you have, the easier your edit will be. A famous director once said to me, "You can't edit what you don't have. You can only edit what was shot." To which I would add: "You can only edit what you can find." So be organized.

2. Less is more.

   It is far more common to leave your shots too long than to make them too short. The truth is, *there is always something you can lose*—whether your shots are going on too long or you have too much coverage providing too many angles on something that doesn't require it. I can usually pull 10 to 20 frames off of *every* shot in my cut without missing a thing. This may not seem like much, but after 30 or 40 shots, this trick will painlessly shorten a sequence by 15 to 20 seconds and generally make it better.

   The hardest part of editing is accepting this notion that getting rid of something good will usually improve the remaining stuff. So don't fall in love with your material: Keep your mind on the *whole* and not any of the individual shots.

3. Don't worry about art.

   In general, don't make yourself crazy worrying about the aesthetics of how each shot attaches to the next shot. When you're starting out, you just need to get the fundamentals down. The rest will come in time. This book isn't really about becoming a great editor (although later in this chapter I will give you some quick tips that might help get you started). Becoming a great editor would be a happy result of working with video for a long time.

4. Make sure that each shot "reads."

A shot must sit on the screen just as long as it has to, and no longer. Beginners tend to have problems at both ends of the spectrum: long shots that go on and on, and shots that are too short simply because not enough material was recorded. As a rule of thumb, close-ups can be short (maybe a second or two) and wide shots can be longer (maybe 3 or 4 seconds). A trick to lengthen shots that you simply didn't shoot right is to slow them down with a special effect. Rule No. 7 below notwithstanding, you can slow down shots that move too quickly or are too short to "read" properly.

5. Sound is often more important than pictures.

This is a brain phenomenon that I can't totally explain. The mind can watch jumpy, jarring, and disjointed images, and if the sound is smooth and continuous, everything will be hunky-dory. But the opposite is not true: Noises, blips, and jarring audio cuts will ruin an otherwise decent stream of video. So make sure you edit for a smooth sound track. This can be easy or hard to do, and we will learn about it later in this chapter.

6. Don't overedit.

Computers make editing so simple that you may want to make lots and lots of cuts just because you can. But sometimes a shot is good when it's long. Sometimes there is no reason to go to a cutaway or see another angle. You have to trust your instincts here and think like someone in your audience. When you, as a viewer, want to see something from a different angle or are not sure what you're seeing onscreen, that's a good time to make an edit. But don't edit just for the thrill of it. Too many fast cuts can be as unwatchable as too many long, boring shots.

7. Forget about special effects. Well, mostly.

Don't be mad: I know I told you back in Chapter 3 when you were shooting not to use your camera's built-in effects, since you can add any of them later in the editing process. Now I'm saying *don't bother.* Your editing program's special effects—fancy manipulations of images, color, perspective, motion, whatever—are time consuming to create and are usually distracting and unnecessary to watch. While there are certain exceptions (including some titles, fade-in at the beginning, and fade-out at the end), in general I would advise working without the effects, particularly when you're just starting out.

8. Structure is everything.

Editing means creating a structure from pieces of disjointed video. If the video you shot doesn't have a natural structure, then simply fake one. You can use the elements of filmmaking—the establishing shots, the back-and-forth of a shot/reverse-shot sequence, some details, and a fade-out—to give almost any footage enough flow to make an enjoyable video. The right song from a CD will lend just enough cohesion to your video that you can get away with awfully little and still pull it off. But try to create a structure with the pieces of video you've captured. Without structure, you have little more than a fancy multimedia experience.

9. Clean up blips.

Through either sloppy editing or poor shooting, you may often end up with blips of video only one to ten frames long that interrupt an otherwise smooth video track. When you're starting out, a single frame might seem very short (after all, it's only 1/30 of a second), but as you grow more familiar with video, not only will you notice a single frame, but bad frames will bother you. Good editors will frequently take one or two frames off a shot to make it better. For me, this amounts to watching how objects move around in my frames, and not leaving a shot with a fraction of a movement. You should become sufficiently comfortable with your editing software to be able to trim out a single frame when you need to.

10. You're never finished.

Editing software makes it possible to edit and tweak and fix indefinitely. And because you probably don't have a client or a deadline, you could just mess with your video forever. Often you might think you're done, then watch it again and think, "Hmmm…that shot is a little long. I should cut to a close-up there." This is why I insist on setting (and keeping) deadlines. Give yourself, say, an hour or two, and just edit until the video is pretty good. Show it to some people, give yourself a day or so to distance yourself from it, and then make one more tweaking pass. Beyond that, you reach a point of diminishing returns, so allow yourself to stop. Pull the digital video files off your computer. Unless you do this, you might end up messing with the video for the rest of your life.

Your Post-Production Schedule

Now that you've finished shooting, you will need to dedicate a couple of hours to organizing and editing the material. Just so you have some idea of how these hours will be spent, let's break down a typical post-production schedule (say, Sunday afternoon from 2 p.m. until just before dinner). For the two hours you might spend editing your

20 minutes of material down to a 3-minute video, your time would go something like this:

- Twenty minutes capturing everything into the computer. You can log the material while this is happening (if you haven't done it previously). This is a good time to watch your footage and think about what you want to do with it.

- Forty-five minutes cutting together a first cut—selecting shots from the raw footage and cutting them into a good basic order. Much of the time spent editing is simply watching what you have cut: playing it forward (and backward), looking at the transitions, and feeling the *flow*.

- Thirty minutes recutting and trimming transitions. This means shortening (and occasionally lengthening) shots—take a bit off the end of one shot, nip the head of the next, and generally speed things up a little. I've never seen a first cut that couldn't be improved with some trimming on almost every shot.

- Fifteen minutes messing with titles and rendering effects. You'll have some fade-in and fade-out stuff, as well as a title or two (probably not lasting more than a few seconds onscreen). Even 60 or 100 frames of processed effects won't take more than a few minutes of rendering, in a slow computer. And don't forget to take a break: Rendering time is a great opportunity to stand up, look away from the computer, and stretch.

- Ten minutes dubbing the final 3-minute video to DV tape, and doing anything else.

Why am I telling you all of these things now? First, so that you have a basic understanding of how your time will be spent during the editing process. Your actual schedule will likely vary, but this is a reasonable breakdown that may help keep you from spending all day on a project. If you find that you are devoting an hour to rendering effects, or aren't spending any time watching what you edit, use these scheduling guidelines to readjust your priorities.

Second, they help illustrate the relative importance of the tools and functions that your software offers. All the special-effects tools in the world still will apply only to a small part of your time. Good tools for shuttling and viewing your cut are far more valuable in the grand scheme. Likewise, editing "tricks" can speed up your job, but only to a small degree. If you edited 8 hours every day, trimming your shots more quickly would be considerably more important.

Approaches to Editing

There are two ways you can approach your material. One is to start with the whole pile and toss out chunks that don't work—weird camera moves, blurry shots, poorly framed pieces, zooms and pans. The other way is to start from scratch, a blank timeline, and slowly add in bits that seem interesting. The first is the way you'd sculpt with marble or stone; the second is the way you'd sculpt with clay. Neither is right or wrong, and you'll probably use a combination of both.

Editing, however, involves more than stringing together a bunch of interesting bits of video. You're trying to tell a story, create a little emotion. You want these shots to flow seamlessly from one to the next. Shuffling around the pieces is part of the activity, but that's a little like thinking of sculpting as shuffling around clay: It's true, but it's not really at the heart of the process.

Method 1:
Cutting down (the marble-sculpting method)

The cutting-down method is a fast way to approach material if you *like* most of what you've shot and the order that it's in. In effect, you cut in the entire clip of material you've shot and captured, and then—using the simplest tools possible (like some kind of computerized razor blade and the Delete key)—cut out the bits that don't work for you. This approach is ideal for culling material or doing a fast edit that doesn't involve a lot of rearranging.

Method 2:
Building up (the clay-sculpting method)

If I'm feeling overwhelmed by my source material, or if I want to be more careful in the process, I prefer to build the sequence from the ground up. Start rolling through your video on the source side, and whenever you see a bit you like, mark an in-point and an out-point and then cut the shot into the master sequence. If it is a long shot (more than 3 seconds), you might select the part that best represents what this shot is about and why you took it. Now, as you keep rolling through your video source, whenever you get to the next shot you like, you get to decide if it goes before or after the shot you just put in. Typically it would go on the end, but occasionally it might fit somewhere in the middle of your video. Simply by rolling through your source in the order you shot it, you can file each bit of video in a new order, trimmed down and much cleaner than before.

Your second pass

Whether you choose to build up or cut down, by the end of the first pass you're in the same place: You have a rough cut.

At this point you may consider your work done, or you may want to go back in and tighten (shorten) many of the shots. In this second pass, you might also move a few shots around and maybe delete entire shots that seem repetitive or boring in context. This is also a good time to add music if you want it.

Video Origami

Before this book was *The Little Digital Video Book*, I had wanted to call it *Video Origami* or maybe *Video Haiku*. Not that it involves folding paper or poetry, but there was something about the simplicity of a video sketch that made me see parallels with origami: its rawness, its gestural quality, and mostly about sculpting something small. Few think of origami or haiku as elaborate. A few folds of paper cleverly done, with some knowledge and imagination, and it's no longer a piece of paper but a swan. Or pen just a few syllables, and a tiny poem says so much more than three short lines would seem to make possible. The shooting is the paper; the editing is the folding, where you may (or may not) reveal something sweet, or elegant, or funny. It might take years to simplify your shooting and editing until your sketches are little poems, but it's something to shoot for.

Assignment 10: Compilation Music Video

Before you learn about the relationship of sound to image, let's do a very simple exercise that will allow you to start cutting and have some fun. There are two things to keep in mind for this exercise. First, no production sound is involved—this means we don't care what anyone is saying in the video because we won't be listening. Second, the video will be cut to music, so find a good song on a CD and we will make that our only audio. *(I will demonstrate this using iMovie '08, but it's so basic that it can be done with pretty much any editing software.)*

1. Capture the bedside-table material you previously shot on tape "S1." It should be less than a minute or two long.

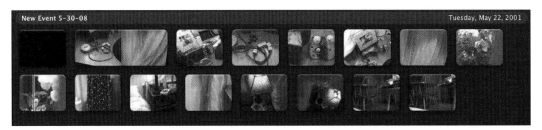

2. Cut in all the relevant shots from your source material to the picture track. (Don't worry about sound at this point; set your computer so that the sound track doesn't play.)

3. Make each of your image cuts 1 to 4 seconds long. They should be sort of like snapshots.

4. Import the song you like from the CD and place it into the second audio track. Once it's there, don't touch it again.

5. Feel free to shuffle shots around and delete any that don't fit.

What you will notice is that the still images cut together easily. The music holds them together. You could easily cut to almost any image within a common theme, as long as there is music but no production sound.

I call this kind of editing project a *compilation video*. These really don't need any formal structure, just a theme. Like a scrapbook. Any assortment of video snapshots (or even digital still photos) will do. The only challenge with a compilation video is that, more often than not, the bits of video you want to compile may reside on different source (or master) tapes, and you may have to do some shuffling to get all the bits into the computer. Therefore, making a compilation video is feasible only if you keep good tape logs.

Play around with your compilation. It's good for practicing some of your editing software's features—capturing, turning tracks on and off, making edits, and moving, deleting, and trimming shots.

Once you feel comfortable with the rudiments of your software, let's get down and dirty with the kind of editing I think you'll enjoy.

"Real" Editing

A few years ago I was in China (teaching kids the material in this book). Usually when I do a hands-on seminar like that, we begin by shooting a little scene to demonstrate the power of coverage and how it works with editing. We often select a couple of kids to play some tic-tac-toe or maybe chess. We shoot for less than 2 minutes. At one school, instead of chess, they played ping-pong. There was a ping-pong table in the courtyard, and a couple of boys began to play. So I pulled out my camera.

I know the rules. I'm going to shoot first wide, to establish the scene, and then move closer to shoot both a medium shot and a close-up. Then move around to get the reverse, also medium and close. Then, any assortment of cutaways I happen to notice. That was the plan. But it's only a guide—the reality is not always so methodical.

As I walked up to the table, the boys were already playing. I stopped when I was back a bit and shot a sort of wide establishing shot, although with a scene like this, it still felt like it was mostly of the guy on the far side of the table, facing me. It didn't feel very "establishing." This was my *position 1*. I held the camera over my head.

Without moving, I zoomed in on one guy and covered him for a few seconds. I just wanted maybe 15 seconds of them volleying. But they couldn't play that well. I hadn't counted on this. Every shot or two, one would miss. So it was challenging thinking about not having a long, continuous segment to work with. The result was that I shot the player on the far side for only 5 to 10 seconds—not really enough.

While I had time, I quickly moved to the other side of the table to get some reverses. Without the reverses—any reverses—I would have felt doomed. So my next shot was a reverse medium of the other guy. This was *position 2*.

I was starting to calm down now. With a shot, a reverse, and a wide shot, I could demonstrate basic editing.

Without moving my body, I kneeled down to get some interesting (I hoped) detail shots that might serve for cutaways. Feet. I always like disembodied hands and feet. Very useful. And once I had a bit of that, I stood back up, zoomed in a little more, and shot some close-ups of the guy's hands playing.

Remaining in about the same location, getting increasingly comfortable that I had the basics, I looked for other cutaway shots. There was a small group of boys watching. I shot them: first wide; then, when one struck me as attentive (he probably had just realized I was photographing him), I zoomed in for a medium shot of him.

Now I turned back around and got some detailed-close ups of the other player's hands, to match the first guy's; but I could tell immediately that I just couldn't keep him in frame this close, so I abandoned this location.

Finally, I began to walk away, to watch this from afar, from some other vantage points. I got behind the watching crowd for a while. *Position 3.* I liked this shot a lot, probably more than the ones of the players themselves. This, in a way, was a reverse shot of the boys watching (you see them from the front, you see them from the back).

And then, as I wandered off really far, wondering if there were other shots of their school that I could use as cutaways,

I turned back around and saw the scene again, and shot what I thought was a far more interesting wide shot. *Position 4.* I shot it medium wide and extremely wide, thinking this could be the opening.

But that's it. Nine shots. Four positions. Fifteen minutes of real time. Two minutes of video. I should be able to cut a 15-to-30-second video from this. I'll show you how I cut it, but as you can imagine by looking at the still photos in the order I shot, even *that* illustrates the scene, tells a little story. This is what I mean by saying that editing can be forgiving. There are many equally good and interesting permutations of these nine shots. This was mine:

I started with the attractive EWS: I felt that you'd see the setting, see the action, but wonder a bit about what was going on.

Then I wanted an MS of the boys volleying. I did the best I could, trying to let them look as if they were playing for as long as I could trick it. Just before one would miss, I'd cut to the other, then to the WS behind the crowd.

NOTE: If I had been shooting longer and not teaching a class, I might have made a video that featured this boy, and sort of depicting the things he was watching in his day, of which the ping-pong was one thing, but that wasn't the case on this day.

I played this shot the longest, partly because I liked the framing and partly because I had a lot of it. But soon I wanted to see the faces of the crowd, so I cut to the reverse of the boys watching—not the WS, but the MS of the boy.

Now, to add some interest, I did a little sequence of close-up shots on both sides of the net, ending with the MS. I chose to finish up with this guy because I had a nice moment where he missed the ball and turned to go get it, and it felt like a bit of closure—it was a natural end (or at least punctuation) to an ongoing game of ping-pong.

I could have ended there, but since I preferred the faces of the crowd to the players, I went back to the crowd, this time wider (since I hadn't used any of this yet), and then faded out on them.

What you should take away is that the order shot has some relationship to the order cut, but not necessarily. And while you never use the same bit of video twice in your cut (it just looks weird), you *do* use the same shots/angles; you come back to a wide shot or close-up sometimes. Scenes of TV are often entirely constructed from a wide shot and two medium shots (OS); no different here.

VIDEO ONLINE: Watch the example Sketch D at http://ldvb.blogspot.com.

Now that we've run through a simple edit, it's your turn to try out some of what you've learned.

The Order of Things

Ironically, the order of the various shots in your sequence is both critical to storytelling and somewhat flexible. In many situations there is no *right* order. Ask yourself when you are watching a shot what *you'd* like to see next. This is the best rule to follow when thinking about shot order. Playing with the order of shots affects the way you tell your story. Here are a couple of examples of mixing it up:

1. The shots establishing where we are don't have to be the first shots of a finished video. It might be fun to start in the middle of the action, but then use the establishing shots to break things up, almost like an insert. (The ping-pong game could have just as easily opened up with surreal close-up shots of their hands, and only later revealed who was playing or where they were.)

2. A POV shot structure doesn't have to be (1) a shot of people looking at something, then (2) the thing they are seeing. It works just as well to show something interesting and then cut to people looking at it. This can create some suspense (which may or may not be what you're trying to do).

3. Most over-the-shoulder shot/reverse-shot combinations can be mixed up with wide, medium, or close shots—particularly after you've established the shot/reverse-shot pattern once. You aren't forced simply to bounce back and forth between the shot and its reverse. That can get boring and eventually difficult to watch.

Assignment 11: An Interview

The shoot: During the next mealtime in your home, interview one person at the table about anything. Hold the camera in your hand and away from your face (or set it down on something solid), hold still, and shoot that one person talking for about 3 to 5 minutes.

After a few minutes of recording, allow yourself to zoom in for some cutaway shots (the interviewee's hands or eyes, other people eating, the food on the table, the room itself). Whatever you do, don't stop recording when you zoom—you want to keep the audio unbroken. You should have one long shot, and near the end you'll have a minute or so of insert material. With an interview and a bunch of inserts, you have all the coverage you need in order to edit. If you want to get a little more coverage, try a reverse shot.

If the interviewee was looking into the lens (and I recommend *not* shooting this way), you'll have trouble performing an effective reverse angle. But if she was addressing you and not the camera, go ahead. Set the camera down somewhere behind her, pointing toward you, and shoot for 10 to 15 seconds to get a reverse shot of you listening to her talk. If this seems too difficult, simply hand the camera to your interviewee, and from where she is sitting have her shoot you just listening, nodding politely, and saying nothing more than "Uh-huh" and "Mmmm."

Before you are done, zoom out as wide as possible and get about 10 seconds of an establishing shot.

The edit: The best way to cut interviews is to listen to the audio and cut the good parts of the interview together, with no regard (at first) for the picture. When you want to remove some part, make cuts wherever there is a natural pause in the speaking—do not cut while someone is talking or *any* noise is going on. This will create a series of similar-looking shots connected at jump cuts. Your video may not be bad like this, but it can be better.

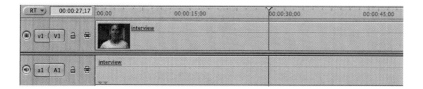

The original 5-minute interview, in one chunk, in a timeline.

The same interview clip, but now with sections removed, leaving three distinct "shots" connected with "jump cuts."

Now that you've done this first pass, find some of your cutaways. Place a cutaway, between 1 and 2 seconds long, between each of your jumps. If you got a good reverse, use one of those just as you would a cutaway.

VIDEO ONLINE: Have a look at Sketch M online: http://ldvb.blogspot. com. In this example, there are two interviews, and each acts as a cutaway for the other, so I didn't need to shoot any special shots to cut away. Quick.

For the bold and advanced: Because your software probably forces you to cut pictures and sound together, during the inserts you'll notice a pause, a breath, a break from the interview. This may be nice and appropriate, but it could result in boring moments. What you really need is software that will let you do the insert in the picture track only, leaving the audio to keep on playing. The insert can go anywhere "over" the jump and creates a visual bridge while not interrupting the sound. It would look something like this:

If your software doesn't allow these *pix-only inserts* (as they are called), don't worry about it. Just understand that this is the next step for making a professional transition from one shot to another.

The Art of Editing

The art of editing could take years and a whole career to master. Not only are great editors skilled at moving the bits around and determining whether or not certain cuts will work (before they even do them), but they are also well attuned to the fine details of image and fraction-of-a-second motion. A good editor will carefully watch a single cut over and over, just to get a feeling for how the shots move together. This may be more than you want to do just yet.

Cutting on action

When a shot is just sitting there—the subject is still, nothing is happening—it's easy to cut to the next scene pretty much any time you feel it is right. But what about when things are in motion? Just like magicians, editors use misdirection to sneak edits in so that you don't notice. Hard to believe? Some people I've talked with don't even realize that the TV shows they watch have edits in them at all.

One way to cut "invisibly" is to use the motion in a shot to fool the viewer's eye. If the eye is following a ball flying across the screen from left to right, there's a pretty good opportunity to slide in a cut. You just need to cut to something else that is moving left to right and is in about the same place on screen as the ball. The viewer's eye will simply move from the ball to the next object. This works because the eye is attracted to motion. As long as you cut to a similar motion, the edit will glide right by.

Similarly, if someone walks in front of the camera and obscures the view for a moment, the viewer will naturally blink. This is an excellent time to cut to another shot that has perhaps (but not necessarily) the same kind of movement going on. Once the obscuring object passes by, the viewer can be quite receptive to seeing a different shot.

Finally, even over all my protests, you might happen to move your camera a little in one shot. In that case, the next shot you cut to should also have a movement, in the same direction, to grease the wheels of editing. You will be amazed at how easily you can make invisible edits by cutting on motions (both within the frame and of the frame itself); just consider where the viewer will be looking.

Nothing is more jarring than doing this wrong, however—say, cutting from someone walking left across the screen to someone walking right.

Even if you're watching the same person and think that it's "logically correct," the eye won't see it this way.

Motion example: Trampoline sketch

VIDEO ONLINE: Take a look at Sketch F at http://ldvb.blogspot.com.

Kids jumping on a trampoline is the perfect subject to demonstrate the power (and importance) of cutting on action. Here's the backstory: One July 4th, I was in the yard with my son watering the garden (and videotaping his fun with tomato plants) when a few neighborhood kids came over and asked if they could jump on our trampoline. I agreed. I began shooting them wide, and just let them jump and take turns for a few minutes. Consequently, I had close (actually sort of medium) and wide shots from this first location. (The jumpers were moving too much to really do close-up shots.)

Then I moved around to the other side of the trampoline for a reverse. Problem was, the tramp was up against a tree and near a fence, and I couldn't get back far enough to do a matching reverse; but I got what I could, trying instead to be more creative with my use of the tree in the foreground.

It was also clear that no matter where you stood, the kids were sometimes facing toward you and sometimes away from you. This might make for difficult continuity, which can often be a problem in the editing, but not always.

Finally, since I expected lots of difficult-to-connect shots, I did a lot of cutaways: images of my son wandering around in the background (both close and far—but usually with the kids on the trampoline in the image); images of the kids jumping but from underneath the trampoline; details of faces, feet, springs, and so on.

At the end I tried one more experiment: I got on the tramp with the camcorder and shot a few seconds of what you see when you're jumping. I didn't think I could use it (or if I could, it would have to be short), but it might intercut with someone jumping.

In all these shots, there was one steady drumbeat: the up-and-down rhythm of kids bouncing. Maintain this and editing is a snap. When a kid is moving down in one shot, the shot you cut to would have to show him moving down also—at roughly the same logical place in the bounce. And it also serves to demonstrate how important every frame is. Sometimes the difference between a smooth and stuttered transition between two shots is simply one or two frames (a difference of 1/30 to 1/15 of a second). Without that kind of fine control, editing can be frustrating.

TIP: Go back and watch the trampoline video again. The matches on action wonderfully disguise the fact that in many (if not most) cuts between shots, the kid who is jumping changes. As long as you figure in the proper bounce, you can cut to virtually anything. If you do that, you can edit kid 1 to kid 2, or kid facing forward to kid facing backward, and so on, and it all works. Even though the shirt color or hair color of the person changes—something that in many other instances would be jarring—matching action is a powerful way to steer your cuts.

A little trick

What if you don't have a real match between the two shots, or what if one is of a baby and the next is of a dog playing on the beach? As long as the two shots flow together with a continuation of motion across the edit, it actually doesn't matter that the images don't match at all. A classic example is in Stanley Kubrick's film *2001: A Space Odyssey*. A bone is thrown in the air, spinning end over end, and the scene cuts to a spaceship, in the blackness of space, but coincidentally moving in the same way. The eye follows the shot of the spinning bone right into the shot of the ship. Presto. But these types of edits involve a bit of trial and error. Sometimes the cuts work, and often they don't.

I recently heard an interview with Steven Soderbergh, the Academy Award–winning director of such films as *sex, lies, and videotape*, *Erin Brockovich*, and *Traffic*. (He's also a writer, camera operator, and editor—just like you.) When asked about his style, he said, "Energy is more important than perfection. Perfection is boring. What's exciting is something that's alive, and something that's alive has flaws. I'm all for the accident that happens on camera."

Re-editing and Versions

It is often said that the secret to good editing is re-editing. Allow yourself time to get some distance from your project; then take a sharp (electronic) razor blade and cut out material that slows it down or detracts from the flow. Just as you do when you're writing, first get the basic structure down without worrying about how long it is, and then tighten it up later.

Re-editing does not always mean making everything shorter. Sometimes it means adding things back in that you took out, or finding a new shot that will solve a visual problem in the video. (For example: In the video of my son at Halloween (Sketch C), how do I get him from the sofa to the doorway? Do I have a shot of him that looks like he's moving in that direction?)

With most editing software, you can save any number of versions of the edited sequence you're working on. It doesn't duplicate the digital video (only the project data), but it lets you keep old versions of the same material so that you can refine without being forced to keep changes. If your software allows it, make new versions periodically.

If your software does *not* let you save alternate versions, I suggest you record the cut as you have it now onto your master (M1) tape. You will note on the log sheet that this is an interim version, but it will be easy enough to use bits of it later, should you need to. (More on recording to your master tape later in the chapter.)

Sound and Sound Tracks

In Hollywood there are three categories of sound: dialog, music, and effects. The sync sound recorded while images are being shot is typically considered part of the dialog track. Voice-overs and narration are other types of dialog tracks. Sound effects involve the addition of various noises to augment the picture (door slams, footsteps, gunshots, thunderclaps). Music is usually one of the last tracks added, as you'll want everything else finished before adding a musical score to your movie.

Professionals often work with two tracks of sound, or sometimes even four, while editing a picture. Imagine if every time you wanted to add a shot, you had to add a picture separately and then add the same exact amount of sound—and if you were off even a tiny bit, all the sound might be out of sync with the pictures. As you have probably experienced, it is profoundly irritating to watch a movie when the sound is out of sync with the picture. Because you don't want to deal with keeping all these independent audio tracks in sync with one another and with the picture, let's focus on a simple case: a dialog track and a music track.

TIP: In your edited music videos, let the picture end a few seconds before the music. This way, the image fades to black, and a moment later the music fades out. This gives a satisfying closure that in many ways works better than suddenly ending both picture and sound together.

If you keep your picture together with all the sound that was shot with it, your dialog track is taken care of. In fact, with some editing software (such as iMovie), it is an advanced function even to separate the production sound from the picture it goes with. In that case, you can still *turn off* the entire track of sound so that it is as if you were cutting only the picture. When you don't have to think about sound, many things get easier.

Adding music from an audio CD is easy in most editing software; it is usually treated as an "import" of the music "file," as if it were any other computer document. By placing this music on its own track, you can control its volume and where it starts, relative to your picture. Never put anything on the music track but the music. It's just too darn confusing.

Add Some Distance

Here's a phenomenon I notice in my video sketches. Videos with production sound are very, *very* personal. I would typically be uncomfortable making these public, even if nothing particularly personal were going on. Take the production sound away, however, on even the most personal video—and add in an appropriate high-quality music track—and suddenly the video is oddly disconnected from reality, almost expanded from the specific ("your family") to the general ("some people"). I am far more comfortable sharing some family videos when they are abstracted with sound tracks. I am certain this is somehow related to the observation that taking still pictures (without sound) is a nice hobby, an art form, and even if the subject doesn't know he or she is being photographed, it's generally "candid." But record audio of people talking, without a camera, and you're creepy, you're spying, you're eavesdropping. The things we say are quite personal, only meant to be heard by those closest to us. Where we show everyone our external facade, few can hear our whispers.

Your Master Tape

When all is said and done, the computer goes away and what you are left with is a DV tape with a recording on it. Now that you're pretty well organized, you know not to record your edited video onto the same tape you used for the original (source) footage. You have a special tape, labeled *M1*, that will be your first "master" videotape.

Master tapes represent both a great deal of work and, ultimately, the part of your video collection you will cherish and watch over and over. I keep many types of video on my master tapes for each project I do. But as I said in Chapter 3, you can devise your own organizing methods that best suit your particular needs.

There are three variations of an edited sequence I like to keep on my master tapes: the rough draft, the final cut, and the protection copy.

You may choose to keep only your "final cut" and ignore the other copies, or you may choose to have two kinds of master tapes—one for final cuts and one for the others. All of this recording is a lot of work (even a 5-minute video might require 20 minutes of messing around recording various versions), and I don't always do all three for each of my videos. So let's look at each of these and why you may or may not need them.

1. **The rough draft.** As I said earlier, I recommend finishing your cut, getting it as good as you want it, and then letting people see it for a few days. Simply record this rough draft onto a DV tape and show it off. This gives you some necessary distance from the project and lets you see how others receive it. Remember, you've been staring at this material, often frame by frame, for hours. No one else will scrutinize it the way you have. They'll probably be thrilled regardless of its quality, but *you* will see things you want to fix. Even if I later go back and make more changes, I keep the rough draft around as a just-in-case backup.

2. **The final cut.** This is it—the whole enchilada, the finished project. Record it to your master DV tape when you're all done and before you delete all the files from your computer. There's no going back after that.

I always record my final cuts with 10 to 15 seconds of black at the head and tail of the sequence. (You can set the computer to add this automatically when it outputs a video.) There's no reason to use a countdown—it's only used for synchronizing the picture and sound tracks, if you must know—and unless you're planning to submit your video to a television network or a film competition, you probably don't need "bars and tone" either. But if it makes you feel important, go ahead.

If I am feeling particularly cautious (or if it's a very special video), I will sometimes record a duplicate copy of the final cut onto a *different* master tape—just in case something terrible happens to this tape. By spreading copies across a couple of videotapes, you can minimize the risk from technical problems in the future.

3.   **Protection copy.** Ah, the ol' protection copy. Mine is a version of my final cut, but with the titles, music, and special effects *removed*. Why bother doing this? Because if you ever want to do better titles or effects, or use a different song, or re-edit later, you can't start from a video that already has them all there, all mixed together.

     Sometimes I go back to my videos weeks or months later—particularly if they are a little on the long side and I want to make a trimmed-down version for my friends. I don't go back to the original source material; I start by capturing the protection copy—the finished video without titles, music, or effects—and cut down from there. If there were already titles or special effects in the video, cutting this down would be more difficult.

TIP: You could record a protection copy before you added the titles and effects. That's perfectly OK. But I tend to keep on changing the video right up until the end, so it wouldn't really work for me. Instead, I finish the cut, record my final cut to tape, then go back and remove the effects and record that to tape afterward. But whatever works for you is fine.

Preparing your master tape

1.   Load a new blank (60-minute) master tape in your camera. Never use recycled tape stock for important master tapes.

2. Bump it for about 30 seconds. You'll need clean timecode on your master tape, just as you do on your source tapes. A good "bed" of black at the beginning (head) of the tape is a start. Never record from the very beginning of a videotape.

3. Rewind the tape for about 15 seconds, so that you are starting to record at about 15 seconds into it, at a place that you know has clean timecode.

4. Make sure your editing software is set up to add between 10 and 15 seconds of *black* at the start and end of a cut. This ensures a little "frame" around the video and provides "handles" for working with this material. The precise amount of black between videos isn't that important; you just want clear and easily managed spaces so that you can record your video to other tapes or get it back in a computer if you want to. My videos are, on average, about 30 to 40 seconds apart on my master tapes.

5. Record to your master tape. This can be through special output options, or be as simple as pressing "Play" on your editing system and "Record" on your connected camcorder.

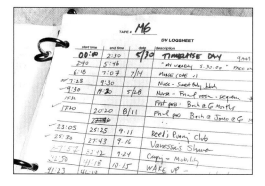

6. Log your master tapes carefully. Otherwise, you'll get frustrated fast-forwarding a master tape to find a certain final cut, seeing what you *think* is the one you want, dubbing it to VHS for your friends—and only later realizing that this was just a draft and not the final version. A good log prevents this kind of mishap.

7. Don't fill the tape. Stop your last video well ahead of the end of the tape. I fill a master tape to about 40 to 50 minutes.

My master tapes, if viewed graphically, would look something like this:

With black leader at the head, a video, more black, another video, and so on until the last video (finishing with black), the tape just runs on until it finishes.

Quality control

Don't be alarmed, but there are any number of ways for a computer to make a mistake while recording video to tape. (I won't go into why.) The most common error is the dropout, where one frame of video gets skipped and a frame of black goes in its place; in another case, a frame "sticks" or freezes for an instant before the video moves on. Sometimes the glitches are stutters or dropouts in audio only.

After I record a tape, I watch it to make sure the recording is a good one. In technical circles, this is called the *quality control* or *QC* process, and is vital before professional videotapes are sent to important people, like movie studios, producers, or advertising clients. For home video, I suggest that you check the recordings of your more valuable works, at least before you delete all the media files from your computer.

Titles and Special Effects

As I've already warned you, you should not overuse special effects in your editing. They are time consuming to generate on your computer, and making them work well can be difficult. It's an entirely different art form from editing.

TIP: When I shoot video of people, particularly for the first time, I try to make a cut to give them. That way, they know what I am doing with the material, and how sensitive (or insensitive) I am being to them. If they like what they see, they will be far more relaxed in the future. (And if they don't, they probably have good reason.) Since you shoot far more than you'll edit, you probably won't do this every time, but try it at least once.

To produce an effect on a bit of video, your computer must do a lot of mathematical calculations for every pixel in every affected frame. Newer computers with fast CPUs can do this math more quickly than older, slower computers, but for the most part the effects are always done "out of real time," which means you will have to wait while the computer renders them. If you don't like the effect you see and want to change it, the computer will have to re-render, starting the whole process over again.

But some effects are not that complicated for computers to process and thus offer a good bang for the buck; I'd like to introduce you to a few that are appropriate for home video.

Dissolves

A dissolve occurs when one shot is onscreen and then slowly (or quickly) disappears as the next shot simultaneously appears in its place. Technically, a dissolve is a fade-out of the first shot with a simultaneous fade-in on the second shot.

The important technical thing to know about a dissolve is that in most cases it makes your shots longer. Frames are added to a shot to create the dissolve, and often those frames are not appropriate to see. For instance, if your shot ends perfectly with your dog "playing dead," adding a dissolve might add the frames where the dog starts to get up—clearly ruining the effect! It's worse if the frames after your shot come from an entirely different setup, and you sort of see a jump as the dissolve goes by. Regardless, just remember that a dissolve might not work well with the material you are editing and it may take time to get right.

For editing purposes, you need to know that a dissolve elongates an edit transition. An ordinary cut happens quite quickly; shot A is gone in a mere blink, replaced by shot B. A bad edit may not be easy to watch as it goes by, but the pain is short-lived. With a dissolve, what would have happened in an instant takes much longer, maybe a second or two. You might think that a dissolve would soften a transition, but it actually draws attention to it. There are times when dissolves work well, like when you want to slow down a pictorial scene or show the passing of time. I find that they are rarely appropriate when editing a conversation.

Dissolves can be aesthetically pleasing and even romantic. But make sure you use them with care.

Real Time

As you learn about computers and video, the term *real time* comes up a lot. Let me define it a little here.

When you dub a video to another tape, it will take the same amount of time to duplicate as the running time of the original tape—thus the copying occurs *in real time*.

If you want to perform a special effect on your video—say, to change a color sequence to black-and-white—your computer might have to "chunk" on it for a while to process this effect. So if processing a 10-second video clip actually took 30 seconds, you'd say the process took *3X real time*.

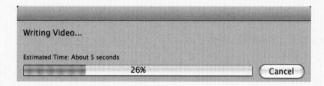

In a perfect world, you'd say you wanted a certain effect and the computer would render it so quickly it would just be there when you played your video. This is described as happening in "real time"—even if it actually happens instantaneously (faster than real time). As long as you don't have to wait to see your effect, it's a good thing.

Fades

A fade is sort of a half-dissolve: Instead of a transition from one shot to another, it is a transition between a shot and black. Shots can fade in (or fade up—same thing), as well as fade out (or fade down). Since fades are basically in or out of black, they are nice effects to use for opening or closing your video, sometimes regardless of what the first and last shots are. So even if your final shot is not of somebody walking off into the sunset, a nice fade-out will draw the video to a good close.

Using fades *within* a video (and not just at the beginning or end) is a stylistic choice that can look quite cool but can be tough to make work. I would suggest skipping all but opening and closing fades until you are more comfortable with editing.

Titles

You will almost always need some kind of titles in your videos. Although technically they are special effects and should be used sparingly, titles add so much that you will want to use them—either at the beginning to introduce something (an opening title) or at the end as *credits* that roll by.

NOTE: High definition does provide the opportunity for smaller and finer titling, due to the significant increase in resolution onscreen, but legibility in all its forms is still critical.

Most important, your titles should be very legible. In general, it is difficult to read text on a low-def television screen—considerably harder than on a computer. TV has poor resolution, people tend to sit pretty far away from the set, and they don't usually expect to be reading onscreen anyway—so a title may surprise them.

Rubin's rules of titling: For all the above reasons, I suggest the following:

1. Titles should be white text on a dark (or black) background.

    Colored titles can be interesting, but the colors can compete with the colors in a background of video. Trying to read, say, a red title over a green background can present many psychophysical challenges to the viewer. On television, titles tend to be light over dark, not dark over light. This is done because bright screens are hard to stare at, and dark letters on a light screen are difficult to read.

2. Titles are clearer if they are done in a sans-serif font like Helvetica (which is said to add legibility to onscreen text). However, I think that the font is less important than the type size.

3. Make your titles large enough to be read by anyone. Point size—the traditional way to describe font sizes—doesn't work well to define titles, as they will be different sizes on different monitors. I won't get technical here; just make them large enough that you can read them on the kind of monitor where they will ultimately be seen, and always err on the side of caution—even if you have a giant LCD display, the video might also be seen tiny, on the Web. Make stuff big. This may take a little experimentation.

4. If your software offers it, add a small *drop shadow* to all titles. This helps separate the title from the background, particularly if a title ends up over video and not against a plain black screen. (Some software does this automatically, which is nice.)

5. Make sure the titles remain on the screen long enough to be read. This is the most common problem that beginners have with titles. I can't tell you how long to leave your titles onscreen because I'm not reading them. But you'll know. Just keep in mind that the viewers won't know when a title is coming, so in the first instant when it appears, they're only realizing what it is; then they may read it slowly. So try doubling the time it takes *you* to read a title—then add a little more for good measure. If you choose to place your title over moving video (instead of a black frame), it will be even harder to read, requiring even more time onscreen.

6. Keep your opening titles simple. If you must add detailed text, put it at the end, preferably over black (keeping the audio running underneath). Sometimes this means a short title at the beginning, and the date, comments, or names of people involved at the end.

7. Fade the titles in and out. Fast fades add a touch of sophistication to titles. Try it.

Motion effects (slowdown only)

Motion effects—the very cool software functions that allow you to speed up or slow down a shot—are important for transforming marginal home videos into something a little more professional. A common shooting mistake for beginners is recording shots too quickly, moving or bouncing the camera too much, and panning wildly. All of these make for gut-wrenching video. A gentle slowdown effect can take any shot and make it move more slowly or bounce less. It can take a teensy shot that's too short to read (15 frames) and make it far more watchable by elongating it to a minimum length (1 second).

I have yet to see *speedups* done really well. Amateurs traditionally use the speedup to take a long, boring shot that they don't want to edit and make it happen faster. I suppose that, once in a blue moon, a speedup can work for you, but it's a poor excuse for not cutting something shorter.

TIP: I like to find a frame of video that is rather abstract, and freeze it (or just slow it down a lot) until it has a duration of about 5 seconds. Then I use this as the background for an opening title. I think it's a little nicer than a plain black screen, and it is far easier to read than a title over busy moving video. It is one of the few special effects I allow myself in the creation of a typical video sketch.

Motion effects are usually described in terms of a percentage of the original speed of a shot. One hundred percent is the original speed of the piece of video; 50 percent is slowed to half play speed (thus the shot becomes twice as long), and 200 percent is twice play speed (making it half as long).

Final Assignment: Small-Moment Video

Shoot a video of just one event, one episode, no matter how small: walking the dog, doing your morning routine, eating dinner. Nothing that takes planning—just whatever is happening in or around your home at the moment. Try to get good coverage. If some action is happening, remember to get shot/reverse shots as needed, and always do a number of cutaways. Stay still. Try to frame each shot. Remember all the stuff I've been talking about for the last hundred pages or so.

At some point during the shoot, record for about 1 minute, paying attention to the sound and not the picture. Listen for "ambience" that fits the scene—the sound of your dog's feet on the ground, rustling in bushes, and distant barks; or maybe the sounds of kids talking, plates clanking, and food sizzling on the stove.

Version 1: With production sound

VIDEO ONLINE: Look at Sketches G and H for a couple of examples: http://ldvb.blogspot.com.

So that you can stay focused on the editing process, don't worry about music; just cut together a bit of this sequence, picture and sound together, with the audio turned on so that you can hear it.

What you may notice is that you are listening to the sound to determine where to make cuts (letting people finish their sentences, waiting for pauses), and consequently your picture shots will be longer than might otherwise be warranted.

Still, this is a great approach to your material.

Save it, and let's try another approach.

Version 2: With a song from a CD

Find a song that fits the scene (or one that you just plain like). Import it from an audio CD and place it into the music track. Turn off the production sound track so that you won't get distracted by it. Now do a re-edit. This will likely mean shortening many shots and deleting others entirely. It's amazing how keeping the production sound can slow down the cut. You may even find yourself trying to make edits that correspond in some way to the beat of the music. Notice how the music affects the way the cut works, how it drives the pacing.

VIDEO ONLINE: See Sketch A online: http://ldvb.blogspot.com.

This is perhaps my favorite method for video sketches. Cutting to music with no production sound can be fast, fun, and incredibly forgiving.

Version 3: With production sound *and* a song from a CD

Once you've mastered Versions 1 and 2, sometimes the right thing is a mix. You'd need to be able to control the relative volumes of each separately, but if you can, try it. I tend to keep production sound very low in the mix, there but quiet. It keeps the video from being too music video-ish; but at the same time, the music masks the discontinuities in the sound in each clip that might otherwise be distracting. It's slightly more personal than Version 2, but not nearly as revealing as Version 1.

VIDEO ONLINE: Check out Sketches C, I, and J: http://ldvb.blogspot.com.

Version 4: With ambience

VIDEO ONLINE: See Sketch L (just part 1, "Waking Up"): http://ldvb.blogspot.com.

This is a variation on Version 2. In many ways it is exactly the same thing. The sound, however, will come not from a CD but from an audio track that you've isolated from a bit of the video shoot—the 1-minute shot you recorded without regard to the picture. The ambient sounds in that shot will make up the "music" of the video.

Separating sound from picture may take a little thinking. If your editing software does this easily, you just choose the audio from the source material and cut it directly into an empty track of sound in your sequence. If you use iMovie, this involves splitting the audio out of a clip. To do this, first cut the picture and sound together into your sequence (generally at the end). Then use the advanced function Split Audio, which will separate picture from sound and automatically place audio in its own track. Finally, delete the picture, and presto—you have a sound-only clip. Drag it up under the other edits to start at the beginning of your sequence. Treat it like a track of music.

The effect of an ambient track is different from that of either sync sound or music. It should allow you to tighten up otherwise long shots without regard to their production sound, while maintaining the integrity of sound in the production. Ambient sound has its place in many video sketches.

Version 5: With narration

VIDEO ONLINE: See Sketch E: http://ldvb.blogspot.com.

This is another variation on the two preceding versions. But now, instead of random ambience, the sound is a recording of your (or someone else's) narration. While some people choose to record the narration after editing to make it fit the images, I prefer taking a bit of actual dialog and using it to narrate what we are seeing.

I use narration when interviewing people at weddings or talking with my relatives. So rather than watching a video of these people talking (known in the biz as *talking heads*), I can see what they are talking about while I listen to them.

You do a narration track (also called *voice-over,* or *VO*) exactly the same way you create an ambient track: Simply pull the sound off a shot and disregard the picture.

As with ambient tracks, beginning software makes this process much harder than it needs to be. Take the interview you cut (from the earlier assignment). Get rid of any cutaways and leave yourself a talking head, with jump cuts. Now take each shot in your sequence and separate the picture from the sound. Once you've done all of this, delete the picture. You will be left with an edited track of narration, ripe for being dragged up under the other edits to start at the beginning of your sequence.

Finishing Up

After you've worked only a few hours on the computer, your project should be winding down. You've created some different versions, you've experimented with cutting techniques, you've output the sequence to a master tape for storage, and now you're in the final few moments before you shut down and get back to hanging out with friends and family.

Compressed Digital Output

You captured your video into the computer and recorded back out at full quality; but video is large, and having a master tape isn't really so great for anyone besides you. The best way to share ("distribute") your finished work is by burning it on a DVD or uploading it to a website. But no matter what your ultimate output option, at some point in the preparation your video will undoubtedly go through a process of *compression* to make the file small enough to handle.

Getting your video from 2-plus GB to less than 200 MB requires what is called *lossy* compression, because image detail and color data are lost in the process. Compressing video requires a special bit of software called a *codec* (which stands for "compressor/decompressor"), and there are lots of ways to compress, which in turn means there are dozens and dozens of available codecs. None is perfect; all have certain attributes that make them better for some kinds of video and worse for others. All offer a trade-off between file size, image quality, sound quality, and cross-platform compatibility. Selecting the right codec is as much art as science. And it is inordinately incomprehensible to the layperson (and to many professionals, I promise you).

While there are many available codecs, some are more prevalent than others—for instance:

- ▶ **MPEG-2.** The "classic" MPEG codec, it is the method employed to make DVDs and is also the basis for broadcasters to get HD signals out to you.

- ▶ **MPEG-4.** Said to be an improvement on MPEG-2, it is supposed to be more robust for low-bandwidth transmissions, and to integrate audio and video better. This is what I tend to use for Web videos.

▶ **H.264.** A variation on MPEG-4, it was originally created as a codec tuned for video conferencing. It is said to work better (look better) when the video isn't moving much (both steady shots and nonmoving subjects).

▶ **DV.** Yes, DV is a codec, and it happens in DV camcorders by design.

▶ **HDV.** HDV is also a variation on the MPEG-2 codec, specially designed for HiDef. Unfortunately, there is a pair of alternatives here (HDV1 and HDV2) being used non-interchangeably by different manufacturers. HDV1 is for 720p and HDV2 is for 1080i.

Because you are always compressing for distribution, it's important that you create and save the highest-quality master tape you can.

DVDs

If you're going to burn your video onto a video DVD, start with a full-resolution original before performing the necessary *premastering* required for DVDs. Some editing software (such as iMovie) will funnel your edited sequence directly into DVD-burning software, without your needing to do much, but most will have an interim step of generating a final video file of your finished cut first.

In the case where you need to make a single video file of your edited sequence, you'll "export" your video to a video file. You want to apply little (or no) compression to this original before you move it to the DVD.

The available file formats may vary but will likely include either Quick-Time or Windows Media, both of which can usually be played on both Macs and PCs. QuickTime (a *.mov* file extension) is the compressed media format of choice for Macs; and Windows Media (a *.wmv* file extension) is likely the dominant video media format for PCs.

The process of exporting a file is usually as easy as selecting the Export function and then giving the file a name. In general, you'll also need to specify the resolution in terms of both screen size and type of compression. As I said, keep this file as unprocessed as you can; the DVD premastering process is going to begin with your video file, and you'll compress it using MPEG-2 into a much, *much* smaller file.

Now you're ready to use any of a number of DVD-building software packages (such as iDVD for the Mac or Sonic for the PC). You'll need the appropriate equipment and software to do this, of course. Then circulate them to your heart's content.

Posting on the Internet (YouTube)

The most instantaneously gratifying method of distribution is to post your video on the Web, and the most popular Web site for this is YouTube.

Because this requires compressing your 4-minute video file from about 1 GB to something much smaller—a typical compression is one-tenth the original size, or 100 MB in this case—it will undoubtedly happen out of real time. Thus, when you tell it to export, the computer will chunk away for 5 minutes or more until it is done.

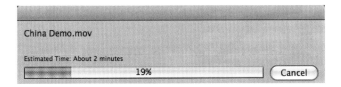

Now you have a copy of your edited sequence, compressed to a much more uploadable size and in a format that other computers can readily recognize. (Technically, DV is not all that computer friendly, certainly not when compared to .mov, .wmv, or .avi files.)

Unlike burning a DVD, preparing a video for the Internet is a two-stage process. First you must export a video file that is (a) of a file format that the Web site can manage, and (b) small enough to be able to upload in a reasonable time and be economical for storing on the Web site. YouTube, for instance, will not currently accept videos of more than 100 MB or 10 minutes in length. (And even if they raise their limit, it is bound to be much less than the size of your video.) Beginning with a 100 MB file will require a fair amount of compression from the get-go.

Aside from codec choice, a couple of easy ways to get file sizes down are to reduce the frame size from "full" (say, 640 by 480 pixels) to a quarter size (320 by 240); I also tend to cut the audio from stereo to mono, as web video is not a particularly fancy presentation, and mono sound tends to be fine. Outside of these quick tweaks, the remainder of the compression will come from selections about codec, and how much to compress ("best quality" obviously compresses less than "low quality"). Here, trial and error may mark your early work. YouTube suggests that you use MPEG-4 compression for your files.

Once you've done all this work to make a video file small enough to upload, the site you upload to may still do additional processing or encoding of some kind (maybe to add their logo, maybe to compress it more), and this will further degrade your video. These are all the trade-offs in the Web world for being able to make videos and get them in front of an audience of millions (or just a handful), instantly.

Deleting Files and Cleaning Up

Digital video files are big. (How big? Four and a half minutes per gigabyte!) Every time you create a video on your computer, you are likely taking up 5 GB of hard disk space for the raw material and the rendered effects files, and a little bit for the project files. Once your video is completed, these media files are of no use. So after you've recorded your final cut to tape and are satisfied that the recording was done correctly, it is time to find the media files on your computer and delete them. If you're using a consumer software package, I recommend deleting the project files as well, since the software doesn't give you any way to rework a finished project. If you're using a more professional-level program, I would keep the project files even after the media files are gone. They take up very little space on the hard disk, and should you ever decide to revisit a project, they'll be there.

Copyright Law

I do not condone breaking the law. If you intend to profit from your video (and don't kid yourself—few people profit from home movies), or if you intend to do anything beyond private screenings and distribution of your creations, you must adhere to U.S. copyright laws. But home video is for personal use, and copyright law is pretty loose when it comes to these private materials.

For this reason, it is OK to integrate copyrighted material into your videos. This includes music taken from CDs or video "sampled" from movie rentals or television. You also don't need signed waivers to shoot people who will be seen in your videos.

But there will be hell to pay if you go "public" with your little home videos if they contain copyrighted material. If you put one on the Web or submit it to the Sundance Film Festival, you've possibly broken laws and may be liable. So I recommend erring on the side of caution and using only licensed music or tunes you have written and performed yourself. If you follow the "better to ask for forgiveness than permission" track and cross your fingers, just understand the risks.

Copyright laws continue to change, and you may want to keep up with them. Now that you have the power of video and broadcasting, you also have the responsibilities that go with it.

On the other hand, you are now a content provider—a producer. You are creating original works, and the copyright laws are designed to protect you. The moment you create an original work, it is technically copyrighted. You could add a copyright notice to the end of your video to notify others that you are serious about protecting this right. Make it readable but small and inconspicuous, like...

© 2008 Michael Rubin. All Rights Reserved.

People you give your videos to do not have the right to copy, sell, or distribute them without your expressed permission. Take this right seriously.

The Hobbyist Videographer

I am a hobbyist videographer, with a *mostly* unvideoed life but punctuated by moments of intense coverage. So use my experience as a yardstick, if you'd like. Just looking at the past four years while I was a busy professional, I shot a total of:

2008	8 hours
2007	5 hours
2006	8 hours
2005	13 hours

When my kids were younger, I shot more—18 hours in 2004, 20 hours in 2003. I think people would say they wouldn't be surprised to see me shooting at any random moment, but they also wouldn't say I am always shooting. Five hours of video in a year represents, and

NOTE: There is one alternative to the traditional copyright; called a "Creative Commons License" (and designated with a *CC* in a circle rather than one *C*), it designates that you retain some rights, but not all rights, and you can specify what those right are. For instance, you can allow others to distribute your work, as long as it isn't for profit. Or you can allow others to make derivative works as long as you are credited, and so on. More and more creative works are showing up with the CC license, often considered a more sane and appropriate kind of ownership. Visit Creative Commons (http://creativecommons.org) for more information.

I'm guessing, material for perhaps 20 to 30 scenes per year, two or three a month (or more often, none for a few months, then a lot for a couple months).

You don't have to do it very often to enjoy doing it, although practice makes it easier and often more fun. Practice on the photography side (holding still, framing and composition, getting useful coverage) and practice on the editing side (cutting on action, smoothing out sound, making it flow together). But the journey's the thing, of course, and this is no different.

Your Next Steps

Once you're comfortable with making sketches, there are a number of ways you could go to push yourself to the next level. Here are a few variations on the basic sketch you might think about.

Complexity

The most obvious next step is being willing to deal with more complex subjects and more material. You might, for instance, allow yourself 30, 40, or even 60 minutes of source material for your sketches, knowing full well that each additional minute of source requires 5 or more minutes of post-production to manage. Similarly, you could give yourself more time in post-production simply to refine your edits further.

Shooting

Some random shots you have recorded might be useful "stock" footage for other sketches, sometimes separated by days or years. For instance, I shot a sketch many years ago of my brother-in-law flying a little plane over our house. He dipped his wings, the kids waved—typical stuff. A few years later, I had an opportunity to fly in a little plane and buzz my own house. I shot the neighborhood, the ocean, and so on. Because I maintain good logbooks and have a reasonable memory for such things, I knew I could probably integrate some of this material. How fun to have shots both looking down from a plane and looking up to a plane, from which to edit. This kind of forward and nonlinear thinking can occasionally produce some fantastic moments in your sketches.

Technology

Work with better (and higher-resolution) camcoders, as well as more sophisticated editing software. Where it might not have made sense on day 1, it is easy to see how you can make your sketches look better and be more complex through the use of advanced tools. That being said, I am still moving slowly into HiDef, and even though I can use professional editing tools, I opt for simpler software day to day.

Content

Think about shooting a wider range of topics—expanding from home videos to small documentaries on topics that interest you—local political issues, business-related sketches (training, promotions, and so on). And if documentaries aren't your style, try scripting your own entertaining short films.

After making sketches for almost a decade, the most interesting opportunity that has arisen has been that instead of always building these little sketches, it is becoming possible to aggregate and edit together lots of finished sketches, to tell a larger (personal) story. With hours of finished sketches, you will also have a chance to make a short movie from these scenes. To do this, you'd return a bunch of your finished sketches into your editing software. You wouldn't be re-editing material from the individual sketches (probably), but rather putting them together in interesting ways. Chronological order might make the most sense, but depending on the content, you might pick a theme.

For instance, I noticed over the years that I had material of my daughter dancing in front of a mirror, for her own enjoyment. I have sketches of her doing this at every age from two to the present. I realized I even had unedited material of the same sort, which I had chosen not to cut. But now I can make a single sketch of her dancing—I picked one song and assembled images of her dancing, getting older and older.

Remember: Edits on action are very powerful, so cuts of her in different outfits in different locations can still cut together nicely if you're working from how she's moving.

Sketches are just that—quick, easy, and good practice. But once you feel you've mastered the format, there is no end to the kinds of advanced and complex projects you can tackle. The skills you now have are as applicable to major motion pictures as they are to your home videos.

Conclusion

We made it. Your head should be overflowing with new ideas and new ways to look at your camera and your editing software. I love what video can do—the power it invests us with and how revolutionary these simple ideas can be.

You've put some work into making a video sketch. And like cleaning the garage or fixing the leaking sink, it's a household job that is both a little hard and quite rewarding. A finished video is a remarkable thing to be able to make; in Hollywood people who can do this are in trade unions, and the only way you could learn to do it was by apprenticing for someone who did it. It is an American handicraft. Now you can do it, and recognize that there are a million and one household uses for your skill. Sketches make for evening entertainment, family heirlooms, birthday gifts, and (someday, perhaps) fine art. In many cases, making someone a video is as generous as knitting them a sweater. And it can be more romantic than a dozen roses.

And these skills you've mastered in making sketches are just as applicable to the professional: Add some better equipment and some preparations, and you can make comedy shorts, documentaries, advertisements, music videos, training tapes, in-house corporate communications, television shows, and feature films.

At first I thought that this book, like any good video, should end appropriately:

THE END

FADE OUT

But as I reread these pages and think about where you are in your relationship with video, I think it's best to conclude this way:

FADE IN

THE BEGINNING...

Index

Safari
Books Online

Get free online access to this book!

And sign up for a free trial to Safari Books Online to get access to thousands more!

With the purchase of this book you have instant online, searchable access to it on Safari Books Online! And while you're there, be sure to check out the Safari on-demand digital library and its Free Trial Offer (a separate sign-up process)—where you can access thousands of technical and inspirational books, instructional videos, and articles from the world's leading creative professionals with a Safari Books Online subscription.

Simply visit www.peachpit.com/safarienabled and enter code LTEPCFH to try it today.